Realistic M[ ]

for Violence & Peace

- law
- enforcement
- defense

An Anthology of Articles from the *Journal of Asian Martial Arts*

Compiled by Michael A. DeMarco, M.A.

Copyright © 2016
by Via Media Publishing Company
941 Calle Mejia #822 • Santa Fe, NM 87501 USA • E-mail: md@goviamedia.com

All articles in this anthology were originally published in the *Journal of Asian Martial Arts.*
Listed according to the table of contents for this anthology:

Friman, H.R. & Rick Polland, (1994)	Volume 3, Number 4	pages 46-51
Richard Friman, H.R. (1998)	Volume 7, Number 3	pages 10-23
Levitas, A. (2000)	Volume 9 Number 1	pages 34-55
Nunberg, N. (2001)	Volume 10, Number 4	pages 76-87
Nunberg, N. (2002)	Volume 11, Number 1	pages 68-79
Román, F.R. and García, C.G. (2010)	Volume 19, Number 2	pages 46-71
Romàn, F.R. (2011)	Volume 21, Number 1	pages 40-55
Hobart, P. (2011)	Volume 21, Number 1	pages 72-81

Book and cover design by Via Media Publishing Company
Edited by Michael A. DeMarco, M.A.

Cover illustration

Photograph courtesy of Francisco Javier Rodríguez Román.

ISBN: 978-1-893765-27-6

www.viamediapublishing.com

contents

preface

Criminals, police, military forces, and civilians practice martial arts which often utilize weapons. One major difference is weather or not the weapons are handled according to legal guidelines. This special anthology includes insightful writings that focus on aspects of martial arts as they are practiced and used by different people on both sides of the law.

Certainly most practicing a martial art are doing so primarily for their health or as a sport. Perhaps they have an interest in self-defense, but often their practice methods are not realistic enough to be truely effective. For this reason, Friman and Polland's first chapter deals with the concern for realistic methods for training martial artists, particularly those involved in law enforcement.

In the following chapter on "The Art of Regulation," Dr. Friman argues that the martial arts are more likely to face government regulation when authorities perceive them as posing challenges to the state's monopoly over the means to create and maintain order. In the quest for maintaining order, Alex Levitas shows in the next chapter that martial arts weapons are widely used by police forces in many countries. Applications are illustrated by photographs credited to noted law enforcement pioneers in this area, including Terrence Winston, Robert Fabrey, Roy Bedard, and Robert Koga.

Two chapters by Noah Nunberg examine the practical legal aspects of using martial arts techniques while training in the martial arts studio or in defending oneself on the street. Assault and battery are examined in depth as to potential criminal and civil liabilities that may arise. Specific cases and hypothetical situations are referred to for reference and insight.

Dr. Román and Dr. García write about the scope and legal framework of penitentiary self-defense. This kind of self-defense is defined by the unique characteristics of a confinement context and a very specific regulation aimed at preserving the integrity of prisoners and penitentiary staff, as well as prison facilities. A technical section is also included.

In the system known as Comprehensive Penitentiary Defense, Dr. Román presents techniques which professionals in this field must master and know how to apply when they face any hazardous situation. These techniques go from peaceful conflict resolution, assertiveness, or body language to joint control, immobilization, or pressures.

In the face of regulating martial art practice and weapons useage, the final chapter by Peter Hobart inspects the right to bear arms. Existing criminal laws and recent weapons bans have made it increasingly problematic for legitimate martial artists to own, use, and transport the tools of their trade. This survey of existing state and national weapons laws is intended to help make martial arts practitioners aware of these legal issues.

All who read this book—whether involved in professions of law enforcement, military branches, or as a martial arts instructor or practitioner—will find each chapter of vital importance. We hope you will enjoy this anthology as it provides excellent coverage of aspects of the martial arts that are rarely discussed but have profound practicality.

Michael A. DeMarco, Publisher
Santa Fe, New Mexico
June 2016

notes

· 1 ·

Striving for Realism: Concerns Common to Martial Arts and Law Enforcement Training

by H. Richard Friman, Ph.D. and Rick Polland, B.A.

Figure 1: Shows Tsunemori Kaminoda (Hanshi and Menkyo Kaidan) using the jutte against Mr. Osato, who holds a katana. Notice the foot pin as Kaminoda takes Osato off-balance. These skills grew up in a time when fighting techniques either worked or died as proven on the battlefield. They are simple and direct and maximize user safety as well as possible options. Today the concepts are the same but practice against the sword would not work well in the country's law enforcement community. *Photo courtesy of T. Kaminoda.*

Martial arts instructors and law enforcement trainers each seek to provide practitioners with the skills to respond to events beyond their control. The serious martial artist trains with the attitude that the techniques practiced are efficient and capable of vanquishing the opponent if executed properly. The law enforcement officer is encouraged to train with the attitude that he or she will have to use skills in physically violent encounters with little time to decide upon the appropriate level of force to use. The challenge for martial arts instructors and police trainers alike is to provide realism in training. Meeting this challenge, however, has tended towards the exception rather than the rule.

1

Very few instructors and trainers actually have the benefit of "martial arts" (*bujutsu*) backgrounds as opposed to martial ways (*budo*) exposure.[1] Serious students are immediately challenged to find quality training while seeking to avoid the array of artificial, superficial, or even phoney instruction being hawked as martial arts. Street-wise law enforcement officers often avoid or minimize their Defensive Tactics and Physical Techniques training, questioning the credibility of the techniques being taught. Improper training and poor transmission of skills wastes the time of the student, thus creating a crisis in credibility marked with frustration. The consequences for law enforcement are greater: community liability, danger to bystanders, and risks to the safety of officers and perpetrators.

Although the reality and chaos of the street can not be fully duplicated in either the dojo or the training academy classroom, practice must be undertaken as if the battle taking place was real. Anything less erodes the value of the training.

PART I

In the typical American dojo, a student enters to train, spending whatever time is necessary to obtain mastery of the self and perhaps as a byproduct, self-defense. In comparison, the typical law enforcement officer (LEO) may spend many hours at the range to maintain pistol proficiency ratings but will typically spend less than three hours a year on techniques for physically subduing and constraining an adversary (compliance techniques). Within the LEO's career the gun might never be drawn out of need, but the LEO will probably be called upon on a regular basis to physically confront everything from crowd control to domestic violence. Martial arts and police training converge on the following elements:

- **Zanshin:** Awareness of the situation, environment, and opponent's condition.
- **Maai:** Combative distance judged instantaneously.
- **Kuzushi:** Balance with control of both the mind and the body to be able to execute technique with maximum effectiveness without loss of concentration.
- **Kimeru:** Timing, but also construed as rhythm, entering into a spacial relationship with an opponent and taking his or her timing into account as well.

Many highly acclaimed instructors regardless of art, way, or culture of origin, believe that mastery of these principles, not particular skills or techniques, are the salient points necessary to acquire a martial tradition. Failure to understand these basic elements would be analogous to building a house without a foundation.

Inadequate training unmindful of zanshin will result in the reactive under- or over-estimation of circumstances and/or of the perpetrator. Poor decision making based on exaggerated skills or impairment of technique due to self-doubt confronts both the martial arts student and the LEO.

Trainees learn too late that techniques that worked under ideal circumstances in the dojo or academy under static conditions may offer mixed results in real life.[2] For the LEO this becomes especially frightening because events demand a choice between possible injury or escalating the use of force.

Choices become limited due to the lack of time available to act or the lost opportunity to respond in an appropriate manner. Added pressures affect the LEO, especially when weapons use and weapons retention are always manifest concerns.

Under such circumstances, zanshin, the ability to see, understand, anticipate, and control events, has failed. Kimeru, or timing, has run out because the event has taken on its own momentum. Maai, the combative distance, is closed because the individual is already in a physical confrontation.

Kuzushi is lost, at least mentally, because the surprise turn of events has left the martial arts student or LEO open to self-doubt redirecting the focus of thought. In dangerously real terms, this is exactly what happened in the Rodney King incident. LEOs were taught that an electric stun gun would stop a charging bull as well as any man. It was tried twice without success. Then the expandable batons were drawn and technique and control went out the window as panic and doubt set in.

PART II

Underscoring the considerations of zanshin, kimeru, maai, and kuzushi are the root problems confronting current methods of teaching martial arts students and police academy trainees. Teaching procedures have been standardized to meet administrative or curriculum needs first and self-defense needs second. Law enforcement requires quick and effective procedures to teach a large number of students techniques for use on the street. In both cases, training requires procedures offering active protection from negligence and avoidable injury while offering a lesson plan designed to promote mass appeal and consistency in training. These considerations lead to a conflict between static training and the need for fluid application and thus raise questions about the effectiveness of training.[3] The administrative needs influence the skills being taught. The martial arts practitioner trains by choice. Many LEOs are decidedly unmotivated and look upon the administrative requirements as a routine to put up with until they can make good their escape.

Figure 2: Takauji Shimizu (Dai Sensei, now deceased) is displaying *hojojutsu*, the police tying art. The cord is often used in liu of steel cuffs. Mr. Kaminoda was Shimizu's disciple and senior instructor for the elite fourth division riot police. Many arrests in the U.S.A. lead to litigation by the defendant for injury done to wrists during arrest. Is hojojutsu more applicable? *Photo courtesy of T. Kaminoda.*

Martial arts instructors, even those with a police background, are often trained and molded in a static environment. Transmission of the martial system is taught by rote exercise and specific, inflexible techniques. The teacher requires that the technique be demonstrated within that club, school, or academy. The advantage of this kind of training is that it provides the ability to uniformly judge the trainee's level of skill and accomplishment.

However, a hazard of this kind of training is readily seen within both martial arts dojo and law enforcement academies, specifically, the promotion of the ego-gratification of the instructor.

Credentials are sought and bestowed with little thought for the consequences, thus creating an atmosphere of illusion and an aura of invincibility as teachers perpetuate their interpretations of skills without being tested, retested, and challenged and tested again. Skills are often absorbed in a teacher-student style which promotes blind allegiance and penalizes challenge. For the trainee in the dojo, this parochialism undercuts the students' ability to learn and improve skill. For the LEO, this narrow view can lead to consequences that include the loss of life.

Testing and re-challenging is also undermined by compliant role playing. Trainees walk through techniques under the calm illusion that a skill is being learned which will automatically translate into proper action and anticipated results under real (stressful) circumstances. Slow methodical movements are introduced to the trainee to be practiced within the strict context of a particular regimen. The environment is safe and predictable to minimize personal risk as skills are demonstrated slowly and cautiously. Yet, in both the dojo and the classroom, such unrealistic instruction creates large gaps in understanding.

PART III

Scrutiny of the evolution of the martial arts reveals that a constant challenge takes place between theory and application. Historically, if a skill didn't work, it was killed off on the battlefield along with its exponent.

Although this is not an appropriate mechanism today, the emphasis on feedback and challenge remains essential for martial arts instructors and police academy trainers. Instructors and trainers must become aware of the shortcomings inherent in common methods of teaching. All improvements must start with the teacher in order to be successfully implemented. Feedback must be encouraged.

Figure 3: The author (r) and Mr. Anthony Woodward (l) practicing jodo.
Photo courtesy of R. Polland.

Personal gratification at the expense of training should be discouraged. Training should be biased toward actual application with a conscious effort to make training fluid. Static skills are necessary for safety considerations as well as psychomotor skills development. This is important for imprinting the movement. But many trainers fail to turn up the heat and introduce the unexpected to the training regimen.

The serious martial arts student can take a lesson from the law enforcement officer about the risks of complacency. The attitude that there is always the unexpected helps to keep law enforcement officers alive. A lackadaisical approach to training in which the student knows there is little risk of personal injury can be avoided by embracing more fluid training methods. Perhaps the most basic lesson is to devote more time to teaching partners to be less compliant. Instructors can also change the maai to challenge the student's kimeru or provide distractions to challenge zanshin and kuzushi. Such steps help to develop the overall ability to translate techniques to street situations, which, by definition, consistently defy simple textbook or classroom scenarios.

Skills development should demonstrate a graduated[4] approach which allows technique to be transformed into a fluid response. The emphasis on developing a solid understanding of zanshin, maai, kimeru, and kuzushi is necessary to build a focus on survival-oriented principles and to develop the will to overcome obstacles. Too often instructors rush into the "good stuff" showing this or that technique before a student knows how to stand and how to maintain physical and mental balance or has become aware of the ability to concentrate in a relaxed state.

In contrast, the attitude in traditional Japanese martial arts dojo is to have the student watch and do in a nonverbal way. The student is required to "steal" the lesson from the teacher in order to hone the powers of observation the student will need. This training function also tests the patience and character of the student and requires mastery before the teacher will seriously attempt to teach the skills of the art.

Martial arts instructors can also take a lesson from enlightened law enforcement trainers who are now providing a set of responses based upon a basic mastery of body mechanics rather than being locked into one technique for response to one kind of event.[5] This approach promotes a deeper understanding of technique and better equips the practitioner to move fluidly from one control level to another as circumstances dictate. In short, trainees are taught to master the principles of the technique rather than being mastered by the technique.

PART IV

Many martial arts instructors and police trainers teach specific and isolated skills. Little thought is given to the overall system of knowledge from which these skills are drawn and to the integration of exercises with survival skills. Incorporating these dimensions are necessary for students and LEOs to build confidence and credibly apply techniques under various circumstances in today's street environment. Ideally, spontaneous implementation of these techniques bursts out as a controlled accident. The basic mechanics are initiated with minimal superfluous body motion and the specific skill or technique becomes second nature with little if any thought given. Rather, the exponent does what comes naturally. And should the technique fail, the trainee understands it immediately and flows into a second or even a third technique. As the student improves this skill, credibility issues and self-doubt diminish accordingly. In effect, techniques must become the by-products of proper training.

The instructor and trainer as well as the student must understand the goals being taught. Perpetuation of poor, untested instruction due to improper training or the ego of the teacher hurts everyone, especially in the context of the law enforcement environment. Moreover, although scholastic research and critical analysis of classical martial arts systems turned to by a growing number of instructors and students can help broaden understanding, such analysis is not enough. The fluid, lifelike nature of proper martial training defies intellectual interpretation alone. It adapts, relies on intuition, and pushes beyond the limits imposed by partial understanding.

[1] This distinction is discussed in greater detail in D. Draeger and R. Smith, *Comprehensive Asian Fighting Arts* (New York: Kodansha International, 1980), pp. 90–94. Also see D. Draeger, *Classical Budo* (New York, Weatherhill, 1973), pp. 31–65.

[2] "Static conditions" refers to class training by rote exercise with a willing and compliant partner.

[3] Fluidity refers to the ability to respond automatically to a threatening event by intuitively executing skills without conscious thought while also intuitively assessing the situation.

[4] The graduated approach should culminate in practice sets that allow "real time" random application of skill under changing circumstances.

[5] Federal Law Enforcement Training Center, St. Simons, GA 1993–94.

· 2 ·

The Art of Regulation:
Martial Arts as Threats to Social Order

by H. Richard Friman, Ph.D.

Introduction

On October 15, 1985, the U.S. Senate Judiciary Committee held a unique hearing to explore the question of regulating martial arts weapons. Senate Resolution 1363, and its House counterpart, H.R. 3259, called for amending the U.S. Criminal Code to prohibit sales of such weapons through the mail. Proponents stressed that the measures were intended solely to regulate dangerous weapons. Opponents expressed fear that regulation was merely the first step toward a more extensive prohibition on the martial arts themselves. The hearings generated national attention, with articles in major news magazines, such as U.S. News and World Report, and in an array of martial arts publications ("Mayhem," 1985: 10; Senate, 1986).

Despite this attention, over ten years later the broader question of government regulation of the martial arts remains under studied in the scholarly and popular literatures. Martial arts historians briefly note instances of broad prohibitions such as those imposed on the island of Okinawa, and narrower restrictions introduced by the American occupation five hundred years later in Japan. More contemporary scholarship on the martial arts has devoted little attention to questions of government regulation. The most prominent works that touch on regulation and the martial arts all tend to focus on questions of the martial artist's legal liability in cases of self-defense, teaching, and weapons' possession rather than regulation of the arts themselves (Brown, 1983; Duff, 1985; Haines, 1995: 157–66; Brice: 1994; Polland, 1995: 109–110).

What explains patterns of government regulation of the martial arts? The question suggests a broader paradox of why—despite offering a positive path to personal enlightenment, physical health, and mental discipline—the martial arts have faced selective and broad prohibitions. Regulation is all the more paradoxical in that, as John Donohue notes, the martial arts are more accurately termed "martially-inspired arts," sharing little with earlier combat systems. Donohue argues that the martial arts of today, including aikido, judo, karate, and kendo, tend more toward "avocations . . . [associating] nominally physical techniques with well defined philosophical and spiritual ideas" (Donohue, 1994: 26–31, 36). Similarly, Donn Draeger's influential work on the arts distinguishes the classical martial arts and ways of self-protection (*kobujutsu* and *kobudo*) from the more modern, cognate disciplines (*shinbujutsu* and *shinbudo*). These modern disciplines emerged during the twentieth century with more of a sport focus, and to equate these disciplines with the classical arts and ways is, as Draeger argues, "emphatically false" (Draeger, 1990: 11; Draeger, 1996: 11).

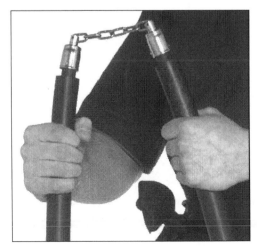 

Such distinctions suggest that government regulation would be more likely to occur during the stages of the classical arts where martial systems were more oriented toward waging actual combat than during the time frame of their more modern counterparts. However, the cases of Okinawa, occupation Japan, and the Senate hearings of the 1980s suggest that government regulation of the arts cuts across these historical time periods. Drawing on these cases, this chapter offers a first step toward a more systematic exploration of government regulation of the martial arts. I argue that the martial arts are more likely to face government regulation when the authorities perceive them as posing challenges to the state's monopoly over the means to create and maintain order.

Donohue notes in passing that all states tend "to create a monopoly on the right to use coercive force and the arsenals that go with this right" (Donohue, 1994: 35). This observation shares a Weberian outlook in its origins, and this chapter briefly turns to the arguments of Max Weber as well as the recent political science scholarship exploring elements of state power. For example, Weber's classic definition notes that one of the core characteristics of the state is its "monopoly of the legitimate use of physical force in the enforcement of its order." The extent to which states have obtained such monopolies, however, has varied over time suggesting that challenges have and can take place. Janice Thomson's work on historical variation in state power argues that state agents seek to obtain monopolies over the decision-making authority to exercise physical force as well as over the "ownership of the means of violence" (Thomson, 1994: 7, 9).

Peter Katzenstein's work on cultural norms and national security suggests the need to look further than the control state agents hold over more overt "means of coercion." Katzenstein argues for also exploring challenges to the institutionalized norms that define collective identity (constitutive norms) as well as "standards of appropriate behavior" (regulative norms) (Katzenstein, 1996: 29–32).

Extending these arguments to the question of government regulation of the martial arts suggests that the arts can challenge the core interests of state agents by undermining state control over the exercise of physical force, the ownership of the means of violence, and the construction of institutionalized norms. The more they do so, the more likely the martial arts are to face regulation. This chapter briefly explores this argument against the cases of Okinawa, occupation Japan, and the United States.

Prohibitions in Okinawa

The most cited instance of government regulation of the martial arts is Okinawa. In 1477, a new central administration on the island introduced a series of edicts that banned the wearing of swords, required all bladed weapons to be stored in warehouses under the king's administration, and required powerful regional warlords to take up residence close to the monarch's palace in the city of Shuri (Kerr, 1975: 104–7).[1] Funakoshi Gichin and Mark Bishop argue that these measures followed the unification of the three warring kingdoms on the island—Chuzan, Nanzan, and Hokuzan—by Sho Hashi, the monarch of Chuzan in 1429 (Funakoshi, 1989: 30–31, 38; Bishop, 1989: 9). In 1477, faced with a successor to Sho Hashi of only fourteen years in age (Sho Shin), Chuzan authorities introduced weapons edicts and other measures in an attempt to further institutionalize the central administration and, in turn, forestall possible challenges from powerful regional warlords (Kerr, 1975: 107).

The ban on weapons was lifted in the early 1600s as Okinawan officials turned to raising military forces to counter the threat of Japanese invasion. Japan's own consolidation under the Tokugawa Shogunate in 1603 had resulted in Tokugawa Ieyasu centralizing control on the main islands, but there was an array of potential challengers. Of these, the powerful Satsuma clan posed the greatest threat.

The clan had backed the losing side in the conflicts leading to the Tokugawa victory and had withdrawn to its traditional strongholds in the southern main island of Kyushu. When the Okinawan leadership was perceived as failing to pay the proper respects to the new Shogunate, Satsuma officials requested that they be allowed to take action. Seeing the opportunity to divert a potential threat from Satsuma, the Shogun agreed. In 1609, the Satsuma clan invaded Okinawa and quickly overran the island's defenses, capturing the castle at Shuri by early May.

As part of the Japanese occupation of Okinawa, Satsuma officials reintroduced the ban on weapons and provisions for centralized stockpiling. A claim found in martial arts books is that the result of such steps left each village with only a single knife, chained to tree or rock in the village center. By 1667, the occupation authorities had shut down Okinawa's official sword works, banned "production of swords for ceremonial use," and in 1699 introduced new regulations banning all imports of weapons as well as training in empty-hand arts (Kerr, 1975: 107; Bishop,1989: 10; Donohue, 1994: 39–40). Funakoshi argues that the Japanese regulations had resulted in the rise of clandestine training in various styles of empty-hand fighting (or *te*), especially among Okinawa's privileged classes (Okinawan, *keimochi*; jpn: *shizoku*).

Drawing from exposure to various Chinese fighting arts, training in these styles took place on a small scale and was centered in the Okinawan cities of Shuri and Naha (Funakoshi, 1989: 2, 30–31, 38). Martial arts books often attribute the rise in empty-hand techniques more to the peasant class, but as Mark Bishop has argued, there is little evidence for such a claim (Bishop, 1989: 10–11).

By 1879, and the consolidation efforts of Japan's Meiji Government, Okinawa and the other Ryukyu Islands were formally annexed as part of Japan (Bishop, 1989: 10). Funakoshi argues that during this period te remained an underground activity, with Japanese authorities having formally banned empty-hand training by the Okinawan citizenry. In the early 1900s, however, the interests of authorities would change. As Draeger argues, Japanese military officials approved te training in 1902 after noting the physical health of practitioners among Okinawan conscripts (Draeger, 1976: 125).

Draeger's analysis captures only part of the story. Japanese authorities initially did not extend the 1873 national regulations on military conscription to Okinawa. Even during the Sino-Japanese War of 1894-1895, local and Japanese authorities expressed little interest in conscription of Okinawans. In 1898, universal conscription was extended to Okinawa.

However, as George Kerr argues, the Japanese authorities set the physical standards of height and weight at a level intended to exclude most potential Okinawan conscripts (Kerr, 1975: 418, 459–62). In 1902, things began to change. As Draeger notes, the Japanese authorities made te training compulsory in Okinawan schools. This step was followed in the early 1910s by the introduction of a broader socialization program aimed at encouraging greater

Okinawan support for Japan, and a relaxation of the use of physical requirements that had limited the number of Okinawan conscripts (Kerr, 1975: 418, 459–62; Draeger, 1996: 125). By the 1920s, the status of Okinawan empty-hand arts had changed to the point where Funakoshi was officially introducing karate to government officials and martial arts practitioners in Japan (Draeger, 1996: 125).

In sum, the Okinawan case reveals that the regulation of early martial systems stemmed from the threats they posed to state control over the exercise of physical force; the ownership of the means of violence; and, to a lesser extent, the construction of institutionalized (constitutive and regulative) norms. By 1477, Okinawa as a centralized kingdom was less than fifty years old. Moreover, the new ruler was a boy of fourteen. In this context, regional warlords and their armed retainers posed a potential threat to the central administration's control over the exercise of force and ownership of the means of violence. Moreover, the potential for a return to the days of three warring kingdoms on the island placed the administration's efforts to construct the constitutive norms of "being Okinawan" at risk. During the early 1600s, in an effort to protect the island from Japanese invasion, Okinawan authorities eased the restrictions on bladed weapons and sought to field a military force trained in their use but with limited effect.

Japanese authorities expanded the prohibitions on the Okinawan combat systems as a means of consolidating their monopoly over the exercise and ownership of the means of violence in an occupied territory. New regulations for Okinawans—prohibiting weapons use (both practical and ceremonial) and empty-hand training also were introduced to further consolidate state control. Japanese restrictions on what had become Okinawan martial arts eased during the early 1900s when authorities encouraged the arts as a means to enhance the effectiveness of Okinawan conscripts in the service of the Japanese state. By the early 1920s, Okinawan martial arts were being integrated under state auspices into Japan.

The U.S. Occupation

The early years of the U.S. occupation of Japan offers a second case where the martial arts faced extensive regulation. Office of the Supreme Commander of the Allied Powers (SCAP) officials imposed a ban on the martial arts, arguing that they had played an integral role in fostering the nationalist and expansionist ideology of wartime Japan. The ban lasted from 1945 to 1948. The reasons for the ban as well as the reasons SCAP authorities had for lifting it support the argument that insights into the regulation of the martial arts lie in exploring the challenges the arts pose to the state.

By the late nineteenth century, the Meiji Government had largely coopted the martial arts into the service of the state. From the relative peace of the Tokugawa Shogunate through the Meiji Restoration, martial training in Japan had experienced a transition from combat systems to more martially inspired arts. As Donohue notes, this transition shifted emphasis more to the spiritual and moral aspects to be obtained through martial training in arts such as kendo and judo (Donohue, 1994: 37–39). From a broader political standpoint, the Meiji Government also completed the dissolution of the samurai as a separate sociopolitical class through the use of official edicts such as those banning the traditional wearing of two swords and discontinuing the samurai's "hereditary pensions and allowances." As these edicts provoked a backlash, the Meiji Government turned to conscripted peasant troops to crush the Satsuma samurai rebellion in 1877 (Draeger, 1996: 28–31).

To further consolidate its position, the Meiji Government turned to promulgating a state philosophy centered on the emperor, a state religion, formalized education, and a broader idealized code of bushido that stressed the idea of "self-effacement to promote greater national harmony" (Draeger, 1996: 29–32). The year 1895 saw the state establishment of the Greater Japan Martial Virtues Association (*Dai Nippon Butokukai*) in Kyoto to "maintain the classical martial disciplines." Four years later, the Martial Virtues Hall (*Butokuden*) was constructed for training in the arts and to increase the popularity of judo and kendo among the general population. In 1911, the Education Ministry "made training in judo and kendo compulsory" in all Japanese schools and also established the Greater Japan Martial Virtues Association Martial Arts Specialty School (*Dai Nippon Butokukai Bujutsu Semmon Gakko*). These trends continued with the onset of the Showa era in the late-1920s. Under the pressures of Japan's increasing militarization during the 1930s, the Education Ministry redefined bushido more in terms of loyalty and patriotism and relied on the Butokukai to maintain standards for compulsory judo and kendo training in the Japanese schools (Draeger, 1996:

35, 45–47; Snyder, 1991: 131–132).

From the standpoint of U.S. occupation authorities in 1945, the martial arts of Japan were of concern more for the norms they appeared to inculcate than any challenge they posed to SCAP's control over the immediate exercise of physical force or the ownership of the means of violence. Japan's defeat, the impact of the public admission of that defeat by the emperor, and the occupation's emphasis on demilitarization (of the police as well as the military) facilitated SCAP's consolidation of control. The Japanese military and police force were disarmed; demobilized; and, in the case of the police, decentralized. Arms production facilities were closed and military bases destroyed. To a lesser extent, business and government officials identified as holding more militaristic tendencies were purged.[2]

To facilitate democratization, SCAP officials turned to modifying or eliminating "every law and institution that stood in the way" (Reischauer, 1965: 253).

It is in this context that occupation authorities turned to imposing regulations on the martial arts. Draeger notes that institutions perceived as contributing to Japan's militarism, such as the Butokukai and "its affiliates," were closed. In addition, training in those martial arts perceived as central to the Education Ministry's inculcation of bushido such as judo and kendo was prohibited. Karate was the major exception to the SCAP prohibitions. Draeger argues that karate simply "escaped detection" as a source of the modern martial ways. In contrast, Donohue suggests that the omission of karate in the prohibitions reflected more a perception among SCAP officials that the art was both relatively new to Japan and non-Japanese in its origins (Draeger, 1996: 48–49; Donohue, 1994: 41–42).

During the late-1940s, the occupation authorities reversed course. Growing concerns with communism in Europe as well as East Asia sparked a broader shift in occupation policies for Japan that also had ramifications for the martial arts. Domestic political stability and economic recovery began to overshadow demilitarization and democratization as the occupation's primary goals. The Japanese police force had been severely weakened by the initial stages of the occupation. Undermanned and unarmed, the police were little match for the rise of Japanese, Korean, and Chinese crime groups vying for control over postwar black markets. Nor were the police in any condition to respond to occupation interest in curtailing the rising strength of organized labor (Friman, 1996a: 64–71).

In 1947, occupation authorities began to reintroduce the martial arts as a means to enhance the power of the postwar Japanese state. Specifically,

SCAP took a number of steps to strengthen the Japanese police, including the reintroduction of training in self-defense tactics. In 1948, occupation authorities reintroduced kendo and judo training for the police and allowed its broader reintroduction as an acceptable sport. With the Korean war, SCAP officials accelerated these efforts, reopening the Butokukai in 1950 and the Butokuden in 1952, and further emphasizing training in the arts for the police and for members of what would become the Japanese Self-Defense Forces in 1954.

In short, the U.S. occupation case reveals that the regulation of the martial arts stemmed primarily from the perceived threat they posed to the construction of institutionalized norms and less from any threat they posed to state control over the exercise of physical force or the ownership of the means of violence. As part of a broader strategy of democratization, occupation authorities attempted to reconstruct the constitutive and regulative norms of the Japanese. To do so, authorities closed institutions perceived as inculcating militarism such as the Butokuden and the Butokukai. Training in arts promoted earlier by the Education Ministry such as judo and kendo was prohibited.

Beginning in 1947, however, occupation authorities reintroduced a different version of the martial arts in the service of the post-war Japanese state. On the one hand, renewed training in the arts was intended to increase the practical effectiveness of state enforcement agents such as the police and what would become Japan's new military. On the other hand, as Donohue and Draeger accurately note, the broader "postwar rehabilitation of the martial arts" placed greater emphasis on the sport aspects of the arts as well as their "pacific, philosophical interpretations" (Draeger, 1996: 51; Donohue, 1994: 89; Friman, 1996b: 10–19).

The Martial Arts in the United States

In contrast to the cases of Okinawa and Japan, the martial arts have faced relatively limited regulation in the United States. This pattern reflects the influential role of state agents in their introduction and the prominence of a relatively sports oriented as opposed to a more nationalistic or militaristic version of the arts. As such, the martial arts have posed little threat to either undermine state control over those who may utilize these arts or the social mechanisms of law and order.

The initial introduction of martial arts into the United States took place during the early 1900s. In 1902, a representative from the Kodokan toured the United States offering "demonstrations and lessons" in judo to an array of students including Theodore Roosevelt (Hickok, 1977: 296). Daniel Rosenberg writes of the popularity of judo "among Japanese immigrants after the 1920s" (Rosenberg, 1995: 19). Tapping into this popularity, Kano Jigoro, the founder of the Kodokan, came to the United States in 1932 and organized several local judo associations . . . [comprised] largely of Japanese-Americans" (Hickok, 1977: 296). Yet, Rosenberg notes that, by the early 1940s, the broader association of judo with Japan, and the practicing of judo by Japanese internees, resulted in concerns expressed in Congress that the art was un-American even as American marines were being trained in its use (Hickok, 1977: 296; Rosenberg, 1995: 19).

The primary wave of the martial arts into the United States followed World War II. By the late-1940s, training in the arts had grown in popularity among U.S. servicemen stationed in Japan. By the 1950s, top military officials, including "Generals Curtis B. LeMay and Thomas E. Power of the Strategic Air Command," were encouraging the training of their personnel by inviting Japanese instructors to conduct classes at military bases in Japan and the United States (Draeger, 1996: 49). This pattern was neither limited to judo nor to Japan. The Korean war sparked a similar exposure to the Korean martial arts.

Former military personnel as well as foreign instructors became the primary source for the broader introduction of the martial arts to the American population during the 1950s and 1960s. By 1953, amateur competition in judo came under AAU auspices. By the late-1960s, similar efforts were underway to standardize training and competition in karate. By the 1970s, interest in the martial arts had grown even further, facilitated by the mass-cultural movie presence of stars such as Bruce Lee and the growing popularity of the Chinese art of "kung fu" (Hickok, 1977: 290; Friman, 1996b: 12–14).

The martial arts in the United States posed little apparent threat to state power. Instead, state enforcement agents, ranging from the military to the police, were training in and teaching the arts. Police departments in numerous cities also were sponsoring youth programs in the arts as part of the Police Athletic League (PAL) to facilitate community relations.

Americans turned to martial arts clubs, seeking training in self-defense as well as a broader sense of association and philosophy. As Donohue notes, the martial arts increasingly found a receptive place in broader American culture, becoming "integrated with American warrior myths" (Donohue, 1994: 26–31, 36, 54–55, 89). Regulation of the arts in this context was limited, consisting mainly of local zoning regulations concerning the location and conditions of training halls (Haines, 1995: 161–163).

The one partial exception to this pattern, however, was the question of state regulation of martial arts weapons. Interest in the martial arts surged during the early 1970s sparked by "kung fu" movies starring Bruce Lee and, to a lesser and later extent, the television series starring David Carradine.

By May 1973, *Newsweek* writers noted that a "Kung Fu Craze" was sweeping the country. The only negative aspect of the craze, argued the writers, was the rise of unqualified instructors seeking to take advantage of the new popular interest ("Kung Fu," 1973: 76). By October, however, reporting on the martial arts had changed. *Newsweek* published a second article on the arts this time entitled "Killer Sticks." The article, complete with a picture of a slightly crazed looking practitioner, noted the proliferation of nunchaku following the screening of Bruce Lee movies. The article stressed the dangerous power of the weapon, the growing number of incidents of nunchaku attacks on the police in Baltimore, and concerns over the weapon expressed by authorities in Chicago, Detroit, and New York City ("Killer," 1973: 67).

The *Newsweek* story and the nunchaku's popularity sparked a wave of state-level regulations on possession, sales, and use. As new types of weapons were featured in martial arts movies, authorities expanded the coverage of the weapons regulations. By the mid-1980s, twelve states had regulations in force prohibiting or regulating selected martial arts weapons, such as nunchaku and *shuriken* (throwing stars), while an additional eight states were considering similar legislation.[3] In mid-1985, noting the ability of mail-order sales to contravene state-level efforts at controls, Senator Edward Kennedy (Massachusetts) and eight cosponsors introduced Senate Resolution 1363, proposing to amend Title 18 of the U.S. Criminal Code.

Specifically, the efforts focused on section 1716 of the Code, covering "injurious articles as nonmailable." The House counterpart resolution 3259 was introduced by Representative Olympia Snowe (Maine) and backed by ten co-sponsors. The amendment called for a $1,000 fine and one year imprisonment for anyone who knowingly sends dangerous martial arts weapons to "any person in a state which prohibits manufacturing, selling, carrying, or possessing [them]." The dangerous weapons of explicit concern included nunchaku, shuriken, weighted chain (*manriki-gusari*), and ninja climbing spikes ("Mayhem," 1985: 4; Historical, 1983–96).

Illustration by Oscar Ratti.

Neither the Senate nor the House proposal gained passage. The Senate Judiciary Committee began hearings on the resolution in October 1985. The proposed Dangerous Martial Arts Weapons Act was reported with amendments by the committee in August and September of 1986 but subsequently died in the Senate. The House resolution was referred to the Judiciary and Post and Civil Service Committees in 1985, where the measure also died. The reasons for the failure of these efforts at national-level regulation of martial arts weapons is not entirely clear from either the congressional record or the Senate hearing. Possible reasons suggested at the Senate hearing include Postal Service concerns as to how such provisions would be enforced (given the variation in state-level regulations) and the costs of enforcement versus the actual threat posed by the weapons ("Mayhem," 1985). This paper focuses on the latter.

As stressed by Senators Kennedy and Strom Thurmond, the purpose of the Senate resolution was not to curtail the martial arts. For example, Kennedy explicitly argued that "the martial arts teach values of competition, discipline, dedication, and athletic endeavor that we all admire . . . but the abuse of low cost and extremely dangerous weapons . . . is giving the sport an undeserved black eye." Thurmond also emphasized that "this bill and today's hearing are not intended to challenge the legitimacy of the martial arts as a recreational sport" but to explore the "undeserved reputation that illegal weapons give [the] sport" ("Mayhem," 1985: 2, 102; Historical, 1986: 6). In effect, these statements reveal the martial arts conceptualized as sport that in and of itself posed little threat to state power.

The distinction between martial arts as sport and martial arts weapons was reinforced by testimony by a top Boston police official, who noted that "we have numerous officers in the department who are martial arts experts— they have very high degrees in the black belt—and I have queried each and every officer and that none of these weapons have a place in their particular academy of instruction, and they find no useful purpose for them" ("Mayhem," 1985: 19, 32). This theme was echoed to the receptive Senators by Larry Kelly, owner of the "largest martial arts school in Western Massachusetts." Kelly, stressing his thirteen years in the arts, eleven as a black belt, testified that "martial arts weapons are an excuse . . . a crutch . . . [for people who] do not want to work out" and have no legitimate use in the martial arts ("Mayhem," 1985: 42–44, 48).

Those martial artists testifying against the resolution before the Senate Judiciary Committee or submitting materials in opposition were in a difficult position. To argue that the weapons were in fact legitimate would risk possible restrictions of the martial arts themselves. This dilemma was most evident in the testimony of noted martial artist Jhoon Rhee. As Rhee observed, "I understand that the purpose of the bill is to protect public safety. However, I am afraid that this bill will merely lead to eliminate the martial arts sports period. How do I know this committee might not introduce another bill to ban martial arts for the same reason of this bill" ("Mayhem," 1985: 94). When Kennedy pressed him on the issue of weapons, however, Rhee couched his defense in terms of the constitutional right to bear arms, noting that he did not teach weapons at his schools because he thought "they could be dangerous" ("Mayhem," 1985: 93, 97). In contrast, and at the other extreme, written testimony submitted by ninjutsu stylist Stephen Hayes simply attributed the Senate resolution to a plot by martial artists afraid of competition from the growing interest in ninjutsu ("Mayhem," 1985: 117–118).[4]

Though Hayes' observation might help to explain the testimony by Kelly, it still begs the broader question. If state enforcement agents did not perceive the martial arts as a threat, why were martial arts weapons? Members of Congress and police officials alike noted the risks to children of unrestricted mail order sales, but placed greater emphasis on the use of such weapons by criminal street gangs against civilians and especially the police. Boston officials used an example of how the arts pose a broader threat to social order by stressing that martial arts weapons were used in attacks by juveniles on police during the 1974 antibussing riots. Justice Department officials submitted FBI statistics noting the "increasing use of martial arts weapons by street gangs" ("Mayhem," 1985: 7, 15–18). By the late-1970s, law enforcement officials had also begun to express concerns over the linkage between martial arts weapons and street gangs comprised of illegal aliens (Jenkins, 1978: 758–71; Keane, 1989: 12–17).

Although such arguments carried the Senate resolution through the Judiciary Committee, they failed to move the amendment through the Senate or House. As Bruce Haines suggested, in the broader context of handguns and semiautomatic weapons in use during the mid-1980s, concerns over the potential threat posed by martial arts weapons were not extensive enough to result in national-level regulation.

In short, the U.S. case reveals a relative absence of regulation, with only selective provisions appearing at the subnational level. This pattern reflects the limited perceived threat posed by the martial arts to state control over the exercise of physical force, the ownership of the means of violence, or the construction of institutionalized norms. Instead, the martial arts in the United States have a long tradition of being backed and promoted by state authorities. But in contrast to Meiji and Showa Japan, the arts have been promoted more as sport (and thus in terms of inculcating common regulative norms) rather than as an integral source of constitutive norms. Steps towards regulating martial arts weapons since the 1970s have reflected growing concerns among state enforcement agents over a limited loss of control of the monopoly over the means of violence. However, nunchaku, shuriken, and other weapons remain less threatening to order than the proliferation of other weapons having little to do with the martial arts.

Conclusion

The ways in which governments regulate the martial arts have received little attention from scholars due, in part, to the very paradox of their regulation. Specifically, given the diverse array of benefits obtained by pursuing training in the arts, why would one even expect government regulation to take place? This chapter seeks to fill this gap by drawing on Weberian arguments and the political science literature on the state as an initial step towards explaining patterns in government regulation.

I argue that government regulation reflects the extent to which the arts are perceived by state agents as undermining control over the exercise of physical force, the ownership of the means of violence, and the construction of institutionalized (constitutive and regulative) norms. The broad and selective prohibitions of the arts in Okinawa and occupation Japan as well as the relative absence of either type of regulation in the United States lend support to this argument. The future research task lies in extending the argument to a broader array of countries and historical cases to gain greater insight into the art of regulating the martial arts.

Notes

[1] For a counter argument suggesting that the weapons ban was in fact a myth, see Florence (1996: 87, note 12).

[2] The literature on the U.S. occupation is extensive. For a brief overview, see Reischauer (1965).

[3] The twelve were Arizona, California, Colorado, Illinois, Kentucky, Maryland, Massachusetts, New York, Oregon, Rhode Island, Virginia, and Washington. The eight were Connecticut, Delaware, Maine, Michigan, Nevada, Pennsylvania, Texas, and Wisconsin ("Mayhem," 1985: 57, 85, 196; Haines, 1995: 164–66; Duff, 1985: 89–94).

[4] A similar argument had been raised in the early 1970s concerning competition between gongfu (kung fu) and karate practitioners as the latter sought inclusion into the AAU ("Mayhem," 1985: 196).

Bibliography

Bishop, M. (1989). *Okinawa karate: Teachers, styles, and secret techniques*. London: A&C Black.

Brice, R. (1994). *A martial artist's guide to American law*. Oberlin: Sanshin Consulting International. Self-published.

Brown, C. (1983). *American law and the trained fighter*. Burbank: Ohara Publications.

Donohue, J. (1994). *Warrior dreams: The martial arts and the American imagination*. Westport, CT: Bergin and Garvey.

Draeger, D. (1996, 1974). *Modern bujutsu and budo*. New York: Weatherhill.

Draeger , D. (1990, 1973). *Classical budo*. New York: Weatherhill.

Duff, K. (1985). *Martial arts and the law*. Burbank: Ohara Publications.

Florence, R. (1996). An interview with Uehara Seikichi on the Motoburyu Udun-di Bujutsu. *Journal of Asian Martial Arts* 5(3), 66–89.

Friman, H. (1996a). *NarcoDiplomacy: Exporting the U.S. war on drugs*. Ithaca: Cornell University Press.

Friman, H. (1996b). Blinded by the light: Politics and profit in the martial arts. *Journal of Asian Martial Arts* 5(3), 10–19.

Funakoshi, G. (1981). *Karate-do: My way of life*. Tokyo: Kodansha.

Haines, B. (1995). *Karate's history and traditions*. Rutland, VT: Charles E. Tuttle.

Hickok, R. (1977). *New encyclopedia of sports*. New York: McGraw Hill.

Historical Congressional Record Index (1983–1996). Dangerous martial arts weapons act. (1986, September 29). Senate Judiciary Committee, page 6. Can be found in PALNI GPO Access at Web Site: www.palni.edu/gpo /GPOAccess.cgi.

Jenkins, G. (1978, Summer). Criminal law–weapons–prohibition of karate instruments. *Tennessee Law Review* 45(4), 758–71.

Keane, L. (1989, October). Asian organized crime. *FBI Enforcement Bulletin* 58(20), 12–17.

Katzenstein, P. (1996). *Cultural norms and national security: Police and military in postwar Japan*. Ithaca: Cornell University Press.

Kerr, G. (1975). *Okinawa: The history of an island people*. Rutland, VT: Charles E. Tuttle.

Killer Sticks. (1973, October 15). *Newsweek*, 67.

The Kung Fu Craze. (1973, May 7). *Newsweek*, 76.

Mayhem by mail order. (1985, October 28). *U.S. News and World Report*, p. 10.

Polland, R. (1995). [Review of the book A martial artist's guide to American law]. *Journal of Asian Martial Arts* 4(1), 109–110.

Reischauer, E. (1965). *The United States and Japan*. New York: Viking Press.

Rosenberg, D. (1995). Paradox and dilemma: The martial arts and American violence. *Journal of Asian Martial Arts* 4(2), 10–33.

Senate Judiciary Committee. (1986, September 29). Mailing of dangerous martial arts weapons. Hearing before the Committee on the Judiciary, U.S. Senate, 99th Congress, 1st session on Senate Resolution 1363, A Bill to Prohibit the Use of the Mails to Send Dangerous Martial Arts Weapons (1985, October 16).

Snyder, J. (1991). *Myths of empire: Domestic politics and international ambition*. Ithaca: Cornell University Press.

Thomson, J. (1994). Mercenaries, pirates, and sovereigns: State-building and territorial violence in early modern Europe. Princeton: Princeton University Press.

United States Congress. (1986). Senate Committee on the Judiciary. Dangerous Martial Arts Weapons Act of 1986: Report (to accompany S. 1363) 99th Congress (99–503), 2d session. Washington, D.C.: U.S. G.P.O.

Note: This paper was presented at the Central States Anthropological Society's Annual Meeting held in Kansas City, MO, April 2–4, 1998.

· 3 ·

Ancient Weapons for Modern Police

by Alex Levitas

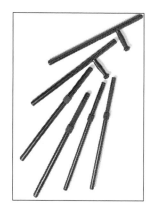

Photos courtesy of Armament Systems and Procedures, Inc.

It is a common prejudice that the traditional martial arts weapons have no practical application nowadays, and are only worthwhile for museums or shows. Despite the fact that traditional weapons mastery is still taught at many martial arts schools, few students can boast real-life experience with these weapons or even assume they might ever have a chance to use them. The weapons of Okinawan peasants and Chinese monks have lost their significance in our age of automatic pistols. They are not suitable for military combat; under most conditions they are too clumsy to carry for self-defense; and in any case they cannot compete with firearms either in range or in deadliness. However, there is at least one area where weapons like the tonfa, yawara and nunchaku (to name a few) have found practical application in our times. With minor modifications, martial arts weapons are widely used by police forces in many countries, not only in those like India or Japan where a history of special police weapons goes back many centuries, but in the USA and Europe as well. Of course, these police forces are equipped with a variety of non-lethal weapons based on modern technologies too: tear gas and pepper sprays, stun guns (including the long-range "tasers"), ballistic batons, net launchers, glue guns, et al. But, as practice shows, the newest inventions may prove useless at times, and then the trusty old baton comes to the police officer's aid.

25

For many years, two kinds of impact weapons were the most popular among American policemen (Ayoob, 1978: 6–18). The first kind was a wooden club 24–26 inches long, often sporting a wrist strap. There were versions that tapered like a baseball bat, usually called "billy clubs" (Figure 1) (similar clubs are still in use by the US Army Military Police), and also batons that were of even thickness everywhere along their length, often referred to as "nightsticks." In some departments, police officers were taught a few baton techniques, borrowed from bayonet fighting and fencing. Although those techniques did not fit the baton well, they were better than nothing, because other police officers receive no training whatsoever. Instead, they simply were handed a baton often with no more instruction than the common joke: "Here's your brain, go to work." As a result, many police officers were using their batons in caveman fashion, unintelligently—beating the suspect on the head until he complied to the police officer's orders or lost any ability to resist (Ayoob, 1978: 11, 88). No wonder that after an arrest in such a manner, the suspect sometimes went directly to a hospital, or even to a cemetery.

The second popular type of police impact weapon during those years was a short club with a metal weight inside. There existed two versions of this weapon as well: the "blackjack" (Figure 2), a solid piece of cylindrical lead at the end of a spring, covered with braided leather, and the "sap" or "slapper" (Figure 3), a piece of heavy steel or lead shaped like a big exclamation mark wrapped in two pieces of leather, sewn together on the edges.

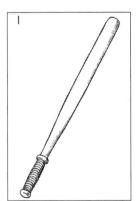

Illustrations by Eugene Arenhaus. Photo by Alex Levitas.

Such batons were the main impact weapon for plain-clothes detectives and prison guards, although many other policemen also carried a "sap" or (less frequently) a "blackjack" in their pockets, usually for a backup weapon or for use in restricted spaces. Such weapons were also popular among street robbers who used them to stun their victims with a blow on the head, and the poorly trained officers often applied them in the same fashion. As a result, suspects were frequently delivered to hospital with brain concussions, or worse, skull fractures (Ayoob, 1978: 12–17).

This situation persisted until the beginning of the 1960's, when two chief factors—namely, pressure from the public and the obvious unsuitability of the weapons for police work—led to the acceptance of new impact weapons, and more importantly, of new training methods by the police. Among the chief demands made on these systems were the possibility of rapid training (within a few days) in weapon applications and a variety of potential techniques for effective self-defense and for arrest with as little harm to the suspect as possible. Since America has no original traditions in martial arts (with the possible exception of firearms) that are easily accessible, it is not surprising that the majority of modern police batons and techniques originate in the oriental martial arts.

The first significant, revolutionary change in the field of police impact weapons was accomplished by Robert K. Koga, an American of Japanese origin, expert in judo, jujutsu and aikido. During his service in the Los Angeles Police Department in the 1960's, he developed a new type of baton, known as the "Koga baton." Like the *jo* and the *hanbo* (batons used in Japanese martial arts), the "Koga baton" is a simple wooden stick (the detail that can be mistaken for a hand-guard in the illustration is simply the rubber grommet [Figure 4] for attaching it to the belt). But, unlike the traditional Japanese weapons, the ends of the "Koga baton" are rounded to minimize the risk of accidental injury to the suspect. Despite its seeming simplicity, this weapon allows a trained user not only to strike, but also to block the opponent's attacks and to perform takedowns or control techniques.

Illustration by Eugene Arenhaus.

In the design of this weapon, Koga tried to achieve ultimate simplicity. In his opinion, the primary purpose of a police baton is to enable an officer to stop an assailant (unarmed or armed with a club, knife, bottle etc.) while staying at a safe distance, and secondarily, to serve as an "equalizer" in case of an encounter with an adversary possessing superior strength or with multiple assailants. A simple straight baton is an ideal choice for both purposes. Moreover, most martial arts weapons are effective only if long-term practice is possible. However, a police officer often takes only a one-day course which is all the training he gets, so he needs to be given the simplest weapon possible and taught only very simple techniques which can be effectively acquired in this short time. Actually, similar batons had been in police use before, and had even begun to replace the "billy club." Koga just removed all grooving, attachments and the wrist strap and optimized the baton's length, after testing different sizes. At first he chose a length of 26 inches (Ayoob, 1978: 96), but later decided that baton length could vary from 26 to 29 inches according to the officer's height: taller persons may prefer the added reach of a 29 inch baton, while shorter officers might feel more comfortable with a slightly shorter variant (Koga & Pelkey, 1995: 181).

The real novelty was a complete change in the training curriculum. The system developed by Koga includes strikes and thrusts (including those performed by both hands holding the baton), blocking (the preferred technique is to deflect the opponent's strike to one side rather than opposing it by brute-force), and takedowns and control techniques. At that time, a real innovation in police baton training was the introduction of techniques for rapidly drawing the baton from the ring in which it was carried. These techniques were borrowed by Mr. Koga from the Japanese martial art of iaido. These techniques were later incorporated into other police baton systems. Attention is also paid to maintaining a safe distance and to selecting the proper target areas on the opponent's body: the primary targets are the suspect's arms and legs and strikes above the shoulder line are forbidden. This set of techniques allows the police officer to defend himself better and to make an arrest without beating a suspect into submission. Until recently, the "Koga baton" remained among the most popular police baton types.

Another kind of weapon used in the "Koga method" is the 42 inch riot baton. Such batons aren't intended for everyday use as they are too awkward and they are used only by members of crowd control teams in civil disturbance situations. The prototype for this baton is the above mentioned jo (48 inch staff), used in a number of Japanese martial arts. Even in the Edo Jidai (Tokugawa Shogunate Period, 1603–1867), the jo was used in Japan as a non-lethal police weapon. In the first half of our century, the Japanese police again started to use the jo—this time as a riot baton. In 1931, the first group of police officers in Tokyo started to study *keijojutsu*—police stick techniques which were based on the Shinto Muso-ryu jojutsu. After World War II, jojutsu was one of the few martial arts permitted by the occupation forces, since it served the civilian police force. When Robert Koga in the 60's developed his method of close-quarter combat for police, he also decided to use the jo as a riot baton, however, being an aikido expert, he based his method of using this stick on the aikijo (or aikido *jo-waza*)—aikido techniques of jo. Techniques for the riot baton in Koga's method includes thrusts, strikes and a few takedowns.

In recent years an expandable type of straight baton gained popularity among police officers (Figure 5). The first police service to use them was the Japanese. In 1961, a 21-inch long collapsible metal baton was introduced, called *tokushu keibo* (special police baton) or *tobi dashi jutte* (jumping out truncheon) (Figure 6) (Draeger, 1998: 140–141). In essence, it was a modern version of the *jutte* (truncheon) (Figure 7), a non-lethal weapon used by the Japanese police starting with Sengoku Period (civil war period, 1467–1568) (Jun, 1994: 237–245; Jun, 1996: 224–229) and, according to some sources, continuing to the end of World War II (Kirby, 1987: 11–12). The first model of the tokushu keibo was a simple baton without any accessory elements, a sort of collapsible version of the so-called bo-jutte. But the next model, the one used by the Japanese police until now, had a side hook, characteristic of what we're used to calling a jutte. Martial arts specialists developed the methods of tokushu keibo application based on techniques of the Ikkakuryu jutte-jutsu school, and this weapon was officially introduced to police service in 1966 (Draeger, 1998: 140–141).

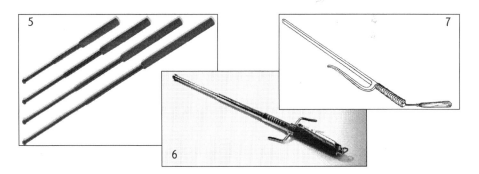

5) Photo courtesy of Armament Systems and Procedures, Inc. 6) Photo by Alex Levitas. 7) Illustration by Eugene Arenhaus.

Today, expandable batons are quite popular among policemen and security personnel in many countries. There are numerous models, the length of which (when extended) varies from 9 to 31 inches (the most popular ones are 26 and 29 inches long). This kind of weapon is much more comfortable to carry (and much easier to conceal), because the length of the baton when closed is no more than 30–40% of the extended length. A regular baton has to be removed when entering a car, so a police officer, having hastily arrived at the site of an accident, may often suddenly find that his baton was forgotten in the car. But an expandable baton is always at hand, and they have won the affection of many a police officer for that reason. On the other hand, an expandable baton requires more time to draw compared to a regular one, because of the additional motion needed to extend it.

The techniques used with an expandable baton are pretty much the same as with a regular straight baton, although the common basic course consists primarily of strikes. Under conditions of limited space (in a crowd, indoors, etc.) the closed baton can also be like a "kubotan" which is discussed below. The efficiency of the strikes performed with an expandable baton is somewhat lower than with a regular baton. Whereas a strong strike on the thigh with a wooden stick would knock an opponent down, an equally strong strike with an expandable baton is more likely to merely bruise. But many police officers have also noticed a psychological effect with the expandable baton. Frequently the sight of the extending baron itself, accompanied by a characteristic "shotgun racking" sound, is enough to make a suspect abandon any thought of resistance.

Illustrations by Eugene Arenhaus.

During the late 1960's and the early 1970's another weapon came on the scene and quickly gained wide acceptance among police officers. It was the baton with a side handle (Figure 8), the slightly modified *tonfa* (Figure 9), a traditional kobudo weapon. According to legend, the tonfa was first used by French police during the student riots at the end of the 1960's and proved to be a very suitable weapon (Asmolov, 1993: 97). A few years later, the side-handle baton was accepted by American police as well. The most popular model was the one manufactured by the Monadnock company and known as the PR-24™ or "Prosecutor", developed by Lon Anderson in 1972 (Ayoob, 1978: 21, 87), and at this time most common police baton in the US (and perhaps even worldwide).

When used by skilled personnel, the PR-24 is much more versatile than a simple baton. When grabbed by its short end, it is suitable for most of the techniques used with a straight baton, while the side handle serves as a hand-guard. Held by the side handle, short end forward, it allows various strikes to be blocked with the forearm without endangering the hand (unlike blocks with the straight baton). It can be used for short forward and backward thrusts when crowded, or to perform wide strikes with the handle spinning in the palm when fighting in open spaces. Various takedown and control techniques can also be performed. When holding a PR-24 by the long end, it becomes suitable for hooking an opponent's legs and arms (Popenko, 1994). However, this effectiveness has a price. While the basic strikes and blocks with PR-24 are natural and easy to learn, the arrest and control techniques are quite complicated and require much more time to master, so that police officers often do not practice them at all. Another feature, particularly important for police, is that the PR-24 is less dangerous to a suspect's life. While the most natural strike with a straight baton is the downward strike on the head, the PR-24 favors a horizontal strike at chest or abdomen height which is much less dangerous.

In the early 1990's, a US-based company began production of detachable handles that could be affixed to flashlights (Figure 10) such as the "Mag-Lite"™ and "Stream Light"™ brands, turning them into a kind of side-handle baton. While not too suitable for thrusting, such "batons" can be useful for blinding an opponent by suddenly turning the flashlight on, and they are about as handy for blocking punches, kicks and baton strikes as the usual PR-24. In addition, such a baton may be used to perform spinning strikes, but these are only to be used in an emergency. The flashlight hits as hard as a crowbar or a lead pipe. Taking this into account, most police departments in the US forbid the use of flashlights as batons, so the detachable side handles for flashlights did not become widespread.

The year 1997 marked the debut of a new kind of police baton with a side handle, the WCB or "Winston Control Baton" also known as SpineX (Figure 11). Terrence R. Winston, an ex-police officer from Norwich, CT, developed his new design to make an arrest more humane and safer for both sides. The suitability of this baton for blocking and control techniques is greater compared to the PR-24, on account of lower impact efficiency. The baton's odd shape is due to its primary use as a lever for performing a variety of control techniques and throws (Figures 12–15). For these purposes, the shape of a common crowbar is the best, as it allows the opponent's limbs and neck to be hooked with the baton's curved ends or "fork" between the forward baton's end and its handle and also provides a better hand rest. The suitability of this baton for strikes is intentionally minimized. Its handle, near rectangular in cross section and resembling a joystick handle in shape, prevents spinning strikes, and the curved ends make thrusts less damaging or destructive. Furthermore, the striking surface of the baton is intentionally expanded, to reduce potential harm. It follows that control becomes the primary technique for handling an opponent. However, grabbed by its short end or by the side-handle, long end forward, the WCB may be used for blocks, strikes and thrusts, resembling techniques used in saber fencing, but unlike a saber, its concave (and not convex) side is used for striking. This spreads the impact across a bigger surface which "disperses" the force of the blow, minimizing the risk of injury. Currently, the WCB is being tested by several law enforcement agencies in the USA and Europe.

Photos courtesy of T. Winston.

The next type of police weapon with roots in the martial traditions of the East is the *kubotan*, an innocent-looking metal or plastic rod 5.5 inches long and 5/8 inch thick, with a key ring attached. Its creator, Takayuki Kubota, well-known in the USA as a karate coach and one of the leading police hand-to-hand combat and baton trainers, proposed it to the Los Angeles Police Department in the early 1970's, and the new weapon very rapidly gained in popularity, especially among female officers. Actually, the kubotan is similar to the *yawara*, also known as the *kongo*, the hand-length stick used in jujutsu (Gorbylev, 1998: 170–171) but the addition of the ring and keys extended the applications of this weapon (Figures 16).

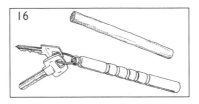

Illustrations by Eugene Arenhaus.

Kubotan techniques can be divided into three basic groups. The first group is represented by thrusts, strikes and blocks performed with the tip of a kubotan held in the fist. These techniques correspond well to empty hand techniques, and a single hit with a kubotan on an attacker's arm or leg may be enough to deprive him of any desire to fight further. The second group is composed of swinging strikes (usually directed at an opponent's hands), performed with a kubotan held in the hand and the keys slashing like a tiny flail. Similarly, the keys can be grabbed with the hand, and the kubotan used for striking. Finally, the third group consists of grab and choke escaping techniques and a few pain compliance ones, including joint locks and pressure point controls. These are pure law-enforcement techniques targeted at arrest, extracting a suspect from a vehicle, control while handcuffing, etc.

Simplicity and immediate availability of the kubotan, along with possible extension of the techniques, once mastered, to a variety of objects in common use (pens, flashlights, et al.) ensured the popularity of this weapon not only among police officers, but among civilians as well. A note must be made, though, that the kubotan is much less effective against an opponent dressed in thick winter clothing. There are also several other weapons that are essentially modern versions of the yawara, as for example the "Persuader™", manufactured by Monadnock and the "Dejammer™", created by Massad Ayoob.

The next traditional weapon to be examined for adoption by police was the nunchaku (Figure 17). Attempts to adapt this weapon for the needs of police in the US were made after the mid-1970's, when Americans became better acquainted with this weapon from popular martial arts movies (Ayoob, 1978: 58; Hess, 1983: 6–7). However, the weapon was not generally accepted. A long time is required to master the techniques; the power of a nunchaku strike easily shatters bones; and in the hands of an unskilled person this weapon is about as dangerous to its wielder as it is to the opponent. All this made the nunchaku unsuitable for police work (Ayoob, 1978: 58, 93).

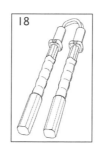

Illustrations by Eugene Arenhaus.

But in the early 1980's Police Sergeant Kevin D. Orcutt, holder of a black belt in jukado, developed the OPN (Orcutt Police Nunchaku), an extremely innovative system of nunchaku techniques, in which the main emphasis is on pain compliance rather than on strikes (Figure 18). This system makes use of specially designed plastic nunchakus. The basic method of the OPN is to grab the arm or leg of a suspect between the nunchaku handles and squeeze it, applying pressure and causing acute pain, allowing a police officer to control even a significantly stronger opponent. Techniques of arrest, defense against punches and kicks with subsequent application of pain compliance technique, methods of escort, extracting a suspect from a vehicle, control while hand-cuffing etc. are all based on this method. OPN techniques also include several basic nunchaku strikes, but these are allowed only as a last resort.

Small, lightweight, comfortable to carry, usable by weaker persons (including female officers), providing continuous control from the moment of capture until the completion of handcuffing, and with the virtual elimination of injuries afflicted on suspects, the OPN are highly rated by the police officers who use this weapon (Fasching, 1989). Nowadays, over 200 law enforcement agencies and correctional institutions in USA use the OPN in everyday practice.

Another version of a police nunchaku is the TR-22 N.S. or "non-striking nunchaku" (Figure 19), designed by Bruce A. Hewitt. This weapon resembles the OPN, but can be used only for pain compliance techniques because of a retention strap which prevents its use as a striking weapon. This allows the TR-22 N.S. to be used even in areas where the law prohibits the wielding of nunchaku.

In 1990, Robert J. Fabrey, a police officer from Brookfield, OH, holder of 6th degree black belt in Kyokushinkai karate and dan rankings in other martial arts, including Yoshinkai Aikido, designed a new police baton, resembling a PR-24 with two opposing handles. The weapon was named the AKD-48.

As the designer claims, the new weapon is twice as effective as the PR-24 (which is reflected by the number "48" in its title) (Roberts, 1991). It's hard to tell whether Fabrey invented the use of second handle independently, or whether he was inspired by the *zhuan tang guai* (Figure 20), the "combat crutch" of the Shaolin monks (Asmolov, 1993: 99, 103, 107). Unlike the PR-24, the new baton is not intended to be used for striking, but rather for taking a suspect down and for pain compliance. The new baton is much lighter than PR-24, which makes the weapon handle more easily and at the same time forces a police officer to use control techniques instead of strikes (Figures 21A-2B).

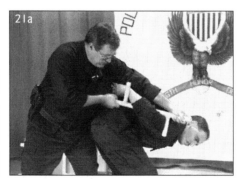

20) Illustration by Eugene Arenhaus. 21a-b) Photos courtesy of Robert Fabrey.

A special system of techniques was developed for the AKD-48, resembling those used in aikido and based on the "no impact" concept. The system includes techniques for arrest, and also for defense from strikes and grabs (Fabrey, n.d.). When applying the AKD-48, the most common techniques are those with the "pistol grip" on one of the handles while using the other for stopping a strike by putting it in the way of the opponent's striking limb. It may also be used to hook an opponent's arms, legs or neck and to hold a fallen opponent on the ground by pinning his neck. Unbalancing techniques and arm locks are used as well. The AKD-48 tactics suggest the constant use of the baton as a sort of a barrier between police officer and suspect, provoking the opponent to grab the baton rather than the officer. As Fabrey reports, the AKD-48 is used by about a hundred law enforcement agencies across the USA, by the US Marine Corps, and by the US Coast Guard.

Finally, there was a relatively new weapon developed in 1996: the RRB, or "Rapid Rotation Baton" (Figure 22). Its creator, Roy R. Bedard, an expolice officer, holder of a 5th-dan in Uechi-ryu karate, used the *sai* (Figure 23), another traditional kobudo weapon, for its prototype. The designer claims that the new weapon retains the advantages of both a straight baton and PR-24 while having none of their drawbacks. Held the common way, the RRB allows the same thrusts, strikes and blocks as the straight baton. At same time, the "horns," which resemble a sword's cross-guard, make it easier to parry an opponent's weapon. This advantage might be of less importance to American police officers who have orders to use their guns in cases of armed assault, but it has aroused significant interest among British policemen who are still armed exclusively with batons.

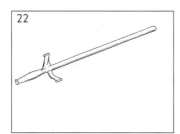
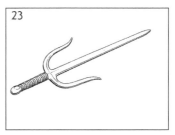

If an opponent grabs a stick, or clinches with the police officer, or even takes the officer down and continues the fight on the ground, the RRB can be turned in the hand with a single rapid motion (for which it earned its name) to the defensive position (Figure 24). In this position the baton, like the PR-24, allows blocking with the forearm (the special design of the handle enables the baton to fit the arm tightly). In addition, this position allows forward and backward thrusts with both ends of the baton, as well as strikes with the tips of the "horns" to be made (Figure 25). This makes the RRB an effective close combat weapon. To be just, a note must be made that the PR-24 can be used in a similar way and is even more suitable for blocking because it fully protects the hand.

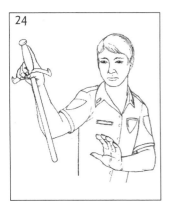 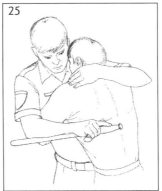 

Illustrations (22 thru 26) by Eugene Arenhaus.

Another feature making the RRB unique among other batons is the way it is carried. Unlike regular batons, strapped to the belt and getting in the way all the time, the RRB is carried strapped along the back, handle down, in a specially designed holster to keep it straight (Figure 26). Carried in this fashion, the baton does not get in the way when walking and running, and there's no need to remove it when getting into a car. The RRB can be drawn from any position, whether standing, sitting or prone, and the drawn baton is immediately in the defensive position. As tests conducted by the British police have shown, the holster design allows the RRB to be drawn more quickly than a straight baton or PR-24 and more quickly even than drawing a firearm (Law, 1997: 13). In case of surprise attack, these split seconds could well determine the outcome of a fight. Currently, the RRB has been accepted by several law enforcement agencies in the USA and Canada, as well as by the London and Dorset police.

• • •

These virtually forgotten weapons have been given new life, coming out of the dojo into the street, and the police arsenal has been expanded by new (really reborn old) weapons. The process of adapting traditional martial arts weapons to modern practice is going on even now, as the examples of the RRB and the WCB show. Other weapons may also be waiting for someone to give them new life.

37

Use of Rapid Rotation Baton

Roy Bedard demonstrates some of the defensive postures utilizing the Rapid Rotation Baton (photos 27 and 28). Photo 29 shows how the Rapid Rotation Baton sits in a holster on a belt next to a revolver. Depending on circumstances, a policeman may conveniently reach for either weapon.

Downward and upward blocking postures (photos 30 and 31) can also be used as ready stances. Notice how the baton protects the length of the arm to the elbow. *Photos courtesy of Rapid Rotation Baton Systems International.*

The Rapid Rotation Baton is often used in submission holds where the baton is used to gain additional leverage against joints. Techniques may be executed with the purpose of gaining control of an attacker and to resolve a conflict without injury (photos 32–34).

Photos 35 and 36 demonstrate police practicing with the Rapid Rotation Baton in indoor and outdoor settings. From basic techniques, their practice must progress to practical applications they may face in their line of work.

Photos courtesy of Rapid Rotation Baton Systems International.

TECHNICAL SECTION

Photos courtesy of Robert Koga.

Sequence I: Baton defense against a straight punch. From a guard stance (IA), Mr. Robert Koga side-steps the punch while gripping the attacker's arm (IB). As Mr. Koga shifts in, his grip slides to the attacker's wrist as he simultaneously strikes to the bicep and follows his opponent downward into submission (IC-F).

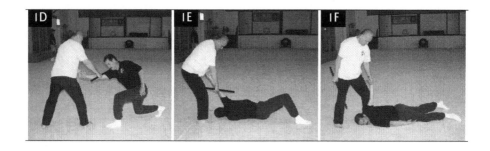

Sequence 2: Baton defense against a low front kick. From a guard stance (2A), Mr. Koga steps diagonally outside an attacker's front kick preparing to slide his right hand under the attacker's ankle area (2B). As the attacker's foot is caught into Koga's right elbow, he brings the baton over the opponent's shin, applying pressure with the use of both hands pressing downward on the baton (2C). The excruciating pain causes the opponent to drop immediately to the floor (2D). Here Mr. Koga can follow-up with a variety of strikes and holds, such as an ankle twist, leg and wrist lock (2E-I).

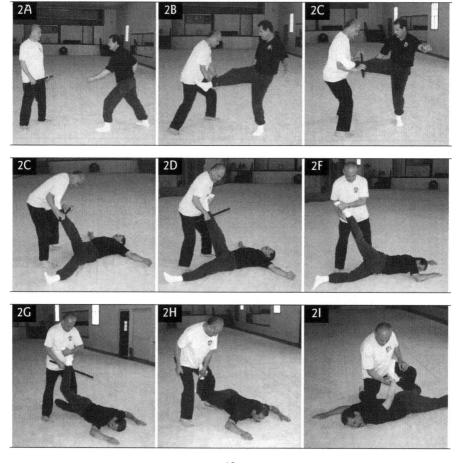

Sequence 3: Baton defense against a straight punch. From a guard stance with his baton in his left hand (3A), Mr. Koga steps back from an attacker's punch and brings his baton to his right side to get a double-grip on the it (3B) in preparation to shift in towards his opponent with a stomach strike (3C). As his opponent buckles, Mr. Koga immediately retracts the baton while changing position (3D) in order to strike the opponent's right leg (3E). The opponent would fall to the ground immobile.

Sequence 4: Baton defense against an overhead strike with a staff. From a guard stance (4A), Mr. Koga steps outside the attacker's downward blow, deflecting the staff with a two-handed block with his baton (4B). The momentum is only deflected, allowing the attacker to become unbalanced as the strike follows-through to the floor (4C). Koga continues the sweep of his deflecting movement, turning it into a strike (40 and 4E).

Sequence 5: Forward attack with a 42" riot baton. Before his opponent can attempt to attack. Mr. Koga was prepared to step quickly into his opponent's defenses with a direct lunge to the solar plexus (5A and 5B). The baton is immediately slid into position (5C) to strike the back of the opponent's left knee in a glazing manner with a forward step (5D) allowing the baton to continue leftward into position to strike once more (5E). This time the waist and arms bring a powerful blow to the opponent's left upper-arm (5F).

Sequence 6: Countering a straight punch with a 42" riot baton. Mr. Koga stands ready (6A). As his opponent shifts in to punch, Koga blocks with his baton, bringing his right hand past the attacker's head (6B). As Mr. Koga steps to the outside, he turns his body and baton, twisting his opponent toward the ground with pressure exerted on the opponent's right arm and neck (6C-E).

References

Asmolov, K. (1978). *The historical survey of weapons: East and west, Vol. 1.* Moscow: Zdorov'e Naroda. (Russian language).

Ayoob, M. (1978). *Fundamentals of modern police impact weapons.* Concord, NH: Police Bookshelf.

Draeger, D. (1974). *Modern bujutsu and budo.* St Petersburg, Russia: Fair Press. (Russian edition).

Fabrey, R. (n.d.). *Official AKD–48 manual.* Brookfield, OH.

Fasching, D. (1989). *Field test of the Orcutt police nunchaku.* Report by San Diego Police Department. San Diego: San Diego Police Department.

Gorbylev, A. (1998). *Claws of the invisible: The real weapons and equipment of ninja.* Minsk, Belarus: Harvest. (Russian language).

Hess, J. (1983). *Nunchaku in action: For kobudo and law enforcement.* Burbank,

CA: Ohara Publications.

Kirby, G. (1987). *Jutte: Japanese power of ten hands weapon*. Burbank, CA: Ohara Publications.

Koga, R. and Nelson, J. (1968). *The Koga method: Police baton techniques*. Fallbrook, CA: Koga Institute.

Koga, R. and Nelson, J. (1969). *The Koga method: Police weaponless control and defense techniques*. Fallbrook, CA: Koga Institute.

Koga, R. and Pelkey, W. (1995). *Controlling force: A primer for law enforcement*. Fallbrook, CA: Koga Institute.

Law, R. (1997). Police impact weapons. *The Shooter's Journal, 43*, 13.

Muromoto, W. (1994, Summer-Fall). Muso Gonnosuke and the Shinto Muso-ryu jo. *Furyu: The Budo Journal, 1*(2), 20–25.

Osano, J. (1994). *Zusetsu bugei bunka gairon* (An illustrated outline of Japanese bugei). Tokyo: Fuyosha.

Osano, J. (1996). *Koryu bujutsu gairon* (An outline of old schools bujutsu). Tokyo: Airyudo.

Popenko, V. (1994). *Tonfa as police impact weapon. PR–24 side-handle baton training manual for law enforcement*. Moscow: Bogoochar. (Russian language).

Roberts, J. (1991, December). Nightstick of the '90s: The AKD 48 police baton. *Black Belt, 29*(12), 36–39.

Acknowledgments

For the information, materials and photos they provided, I would like to thank: Armament Systems and Procedures, Inc. (Appleton, WI); Roy R. Bedard (president of RRB Systems International, Jacksonville, FL); Robert J. Fabrey (president of International Police Tactical Training Academy, Brookfield, OH); Robert K. Koga (president of Koga Institute, Fallbrook, CA); Mandnock Life time Products, Inc. (Fitzwilliam, NH); Kevin D. Orcutt (president of Orcutt Police Defensive Systems, Inc., Denver, CO); and Terrence R. Winston (Norwich, CT). Also, a special thanks go to Alexei Gorbylev, Ph.D., Moscow, Russia, for the help with historical references and translation from Japanese language, and to Eugene Arenhaus, Haifa, Israel for the drawings.

· 4 ·

Civil and Criminal Liability:
The Martial Artists Potential, Part I

by Noah Nunberg, J.D.

Illustrations courtesy of Oscar Ratti.
© 2001 Futuro Designs & Publications.

*Caution: The analysis and statements in this article are not meant as any form of legal advice. They are presented here merely for informative and educational purposes to assist the serious martial artist in understanding potential legal issues related to teaching, training, and self-defense. If you have a legal problem, please consult a qualified lawyer.

Introduction

Knowledge of assault and battery law is an aspect of martial arts training that has been sorely neglected. A practitioner of any martial art should have a general understanding of society's code of conduct in order to understand how to react reasonably to an attack. Furthermore, society's standards are not shed at the door of the dojo with one's shoes. The law has crucial implications within the confines of the training hall. Although legal niceties do not strictly control a person's conduct in the midst of a street encounter or while training within the dojo, a martial artist should take time to reflect upon the legal consequences that may result from using his techniques.

The focus of this chapter is upon the civil and criminal legal consequences flowing from a non-fatal blow delivered by the hand or foot to an assailant on the street or an opponent in practice. The distinction between criminal and civil law is fairly obvious. Criminal liability results from prosecution by the state for an offense or wrong one commits against the public. The primary purpose of a criminal proceeding is to protect the public from an offender by punishing him or eliminating him from society.[1] Generally, the state, as protector of the public welfare, defines criminal offenses in statutes promulgated by the legislature. Civil liability, on the other hand, results from a civil proceeding brought by one individual, the plaintiff, in a lawsuit against another, the defendant. The plaintiff seeks to be compensated monetarily for damages resulting from a wrong or tort committed against him. These two classes of liability are not mutually exclusive. That is to say, the same act can lead both to criminal and civil proceedings.

CIVIL LIABILITY

Battery

The tort readily associated with the martial arts is battery, which is defined as an intentional touching of another person's body without the consent of the person touched. Intentional, in this context, does not involve malice or ill-will but rather is merely the volitional action of touching a person. One may jokingly touch another person and commit battery. On the other hand, if someone turns around and in the process accidentally touches another person, there is no intent to touch him. However, if one walks forward, sees another person in his path, and rudely pushes him aside, there is intent to make contact and battery has been committed.

Consent as a Defense to Battery

As the definition of battery requires, the touching must not be consented to by the injured party. Consent is willingness by a person that an act shall occur. This consent need not be expressly given in words but may be manifested in the actions of a person. Implied consent, as the latter form of consent is called by the law, entitles a person to reasonably rely upon another person's conduct that demonstrates willingness that an act occur. If a person expressly consents to an act, but in his heart of hearts actually has deep reservations, he cannot later say there was no willingness in fact. A party will not be permitted to rely upon his subjective lack of consent when his actual conduct is totally contradictory and misleading to others.

Silence can operate as consent when a reasonable person would otherwise speak. As Professor Prosser's treatise points out, a woman who does not protest against a man's proposal to kiss her may have mental reservations; nevertheless, the man remains privileged. However, a man who stands his ground under the threat of attack cannot be said to consent to the blow he receives from an attacker.[2]

The scope of the consent cannot extend beyond its reasonable meaning under the circumstances. For example, consent to be touched is implied when one goes to a doctor for a physical examination. Similarly, when one joins a group to play football, consent to be touched is implied. It can be assumed that the willing participant is familiar with the rules of the game, which include touching players. If during the course of play the participant has a change of heart, he either must expressly state that he no longer consents to be touched or leave the game. However, consent, whether actual or implied, may not be extended beyond its reasonable meaning. Thus the physician conducting the physical examination may not take indecent liberties with his patient and the participant in the football game may not be tackled with a kick to the groin. Such contacts clearly exceed the scope of the consent given.

Harper and James, authors of a major treatise on the law of torts, state the following in regard to consent in sporting activities:

> It is not always necessary that the person consent to the harm itself; it is enough if he gives his consent to the act which he knows will result in bodily harm. Thus, where one engages in games or sports in which there is a likelihood or certainty of bodily contacts, such as a boxing match or athletic event, he assumes the risk of the bodily injuries which are almost inevitable from the conduct on the part of the other contestants to which he gives assent. "When people engage in a game involving risk, or a game generally safe, but in which accidents may happen, every player taking part in it takes on himself the risks incident to being a player, and he will have no remedy for any injury he may receive in the course of it, unless there has been some undue violence or unfair play on the part of some of the others. He takes the risks incident to the game, and the result of these risks must lie where they fall."[3]

Practical Implications in the Dojo

In the dojo, most contact between students, whether they are practicing self-defense techniques or engaging in free-style sparring, will not justify a lawsuit because consent either is expressly or, more often than not, implicitly

given from the mere fact that the two students agree to practice together. Yet the scope of the consent cannot be extended beyond that which is reasonable under the circumstances. This range of consent within the training hall usually is defined and controlled by the senior instructor of a particular dojo.

As any student of the martial arts knows, the code of conduct in a traditional dojo is quite formal and proper decorum while practicing must be strictly followed. Historically, this can be traced to the concept of *bushido*, the way of the warrior, of 12th century feudal Japan. This oriental code of chivalry strictly defined the proper conduct with which a warrior could apply his martial skills.[4]

Hypothetical Situations in the Dojo

Let us examine the following hypothetical situations. "A" agrees with "B" to practice defensive techniques against unsheathed knife attacks. "B" attacks "A" at "A"'s signal and "A," in attempting to block the incoming knife, is stabbed in the arm. "A" has no action against "B." "A" expressly consented to participate in this training and must assume the risk of being cut by the knife if he blocks it improperly.

Assume that "A" again agrees with "B" to practice against such knife attacks. "B" instead attacks "A" with a long sword. "A," who has not perfected his technique, turns around to face "B" but, before he can say anything, is cut by "B" while attempting to block the long sword. "B" has committed battery, because "A" never consented to be attacked by "B" with this type of weapon. On the other hand, if "A" had seen "B" approach him with such a sword rather than a knife, and had "A" remained silent and signaled "B" to attack him by nodding his head, then no tort would have been committed because "A's" consent was clearly expressed.

Assume now that "A" is attacked by "B" with a knife and that "A" successfully blocks the incoming blade. "B" then remains stationary to allow "A" to practice follow-up counter techniques. "A" does not hold back with his kick to the groin. "B" is doubled over in excruciating pain.

If it is the custom and practice of the particular dojo, under the tradition followed by the senior instructor, to practice self-defense in this fashion, and if "B" was aware of this fact, then "B" would have consented to such a blow. However, the dojo that practices in such a manner is the exception rather than the rule. Furthermore, as will be discussed below, although such consent may preclude a civil action, there may be criminal liability as a result of such a response.

If this last hypothetical case took place in the context of a mainstream dojo, the forceful blow delivered by "A" to "B" would not be consented to by "B." After "A" blocked "B's" knife attack, "B" stood still to allow "A" to practice his follow-up attack. Under the circumstances, "B" would have consented to light bodily contact. Similarly, if "A" began to deliver such a light kick and suddenly lost his balance and hit "B" much harder than expected either by "A" or "B," that bodily contact arguably would have been within the scope of the consent. "B" must assume the risk that, in practicing self-defense techniques, such a mistake can happen. Not only will "B" have learned to avoid practice with "A" whenever possible, he will certainly have more faith in the kick as a defense against a knife attack.

Street Situations

In an unprovoked street attack situation, no question of consent exists. If a martial artist disarms his assailant and inflicts bodily injury upon him, the majority of these types of situations can be defended under the legal rubric of self-defense. The legal concept of self-defense permits a person who is attacked to take reasonable steps to prevent harm to himself when there is no time to resort to the law.[5] This privilege permits the victim of an attack to use reasonable force to prevent any harmful or offensive bodily contact.

Reasonably Perceived Danger as the Controlling Factor

The danger reasonably perceived by a victim at the time of an attack will be the controlling factor rather than the real facts as determined later. If a would-be assailant reaches into his pocket and his victim fears that he is reaching for a weapon, a preemptive strike made by a martial artist would still be protected by the privilege of self-defense even if the assailant in fact had no weapon. The victim's belief, however, must be based on some reasonable ground and cannot be purely speculative and fanciful. It often will be a question of fact for a jury or court to determine if a belief was reasonable under the particular circumstances. Factors such as the victim's state of mind and nerves, the assailant's past conduct and threats toward the victim, if any, and the assailant's reputation will be relevant evidence upon which a jury may base its decision.

The Degree of Permissible Force Used in Self-Defense

The degree of force used to defend oneself is not unlimited under the law. Rather, the amount of force used to defend oneself must be that amount which is, or reasonably appears to be, necessary to defend oneself against the threatened injury. Using excessive force against an attacker will cause the victim to be legally liable to the assailant. An assailant may withdraw after his initial attack.

If he clearly communicates this withdrawal to his would-be victim, the privilege of self-defense ceases to protect the victim if he becomes the aggressor and attacks his assailant. The first assailant, at this point, becomes the victim and the rules of self-defense become applicable to him.

A weapon that is calculated to inflict death or serious bodily harm may not be used for self-defense unless its user believes that he is under a threat of similar degree. The question may be asked whether any blow from a well-trained and proficient martial artist, delivered with the empty hand or foot, could be considered the use a deadly weapon. I shall reserve analysis of this question until the criminal portion of this study. But such an application of the term "deadly weapon" would lead to the conclusion that a martial artist could not meet an attack not intended to cause serious bodily injury or death by using his hands or feet. Consequently, his training ironically would render him less able to defend himself than the average untrained man. Such a conclusion is highly absurd and should not be reached under the law.

However, on a more practical level, a skilled martial artist confronted by an armed assailant should be able to calibrate his blow to meet the attack with a similar degree of force. When there is no time to reflect or to accurately determine the intensity of the attack, then the trained tendency to protect oneself with a split-second and devastating technique, coupled with the natural tendency to preserve oneself, will not be ignored by the law and, in all probability, the force will not be deemed to be excessive. Again, this is a question of reasonable perception under the circumstances and the lack of time to form an accurate perception may be determinative in the mind of the trier of fact.

Duty to Retreat

As is often the case under the law, various jurisdictions have different rules pertaining to retreating from a serious or deadly attack when a reasonably safe route of escape is available to a victim. Courts in the South and West place more stock in an individual's dignity and honor and say that he may stand his ground and inflict serious bodily injury or death when an attack calls for it. Other jurisdictions, including New York, hold that personal honor cannot justify inflicting serious wounds or death upon an assailant and that a victim must retreat when he may do so safely. Generally, there is no duty to retreat when an attack takes place in a victim's home. A person's home is his castle and, when a victim is threatened with a grave attack in his home, retreat is unnecessary before defending oneself.

This concept is illustrated in the New York criminal case People v. Young, 11 N.Y. 2d 274 (1962). In this case, the defendant came upon two men struggling on the street with a third man. The defendant intervened to help the third man, who was fighting against the two assailants; however, these assailants turned out to be plainclothes policemen who were trying to arrest the "victim." The defendant was convicted of criminal assault in the third degree, even though he had a reasonable, although mistaken, belief that the "victim" was defending himself from an unjustified attack.

Courts in other jurisdictions hold that, just as a victim may be mistaken and still gain the privilege of self-defense when he acts reasonably, so too the mistaken defense of others should be worthy of the same privilege. Thus, the People v. Young case would result in an acquittal of the defendant in states that follow such a rule of law. In fact, subsequent to the Young case, the New York legislature liberalized the law and in effect overruled People v. Young by recognizing that physical force may be used in defense of a third person when the defendant "reasonably believes" such force to be necessary to defend a third person. Thus, if the Good Samaritan was mistaken about the victim's privilege to defend himself, a question is presented as to the reasonableness of the Good Samaritan's belief.

Civil Assault

Civil assault is commonly misapprehended by laymen and lawyers alike.

As a tort, assault is distinct from battery in that assault is designed to protect an individual from the apprehension of harmful or offensive contact from another person. In contrast to battery, no contact need be made to constitute an assault. All that is required is the threat of such contact combined with the attacker's ability and opportunity to carry out the threat immediately.

Although no physical contact is required, the law does require a more specific intent by the attacker than that which is required to show battery. The assailant must intend to cause the victim to doubt his physical security and the victim must be aware of this threat. Thus, if a victim was attacked from behind without warning and rendered unconscious by a blow to the head, he would merely have an action for battery against his assailant. Yet if the attacker menacingly approached from a point visible to the victim, and struck a blow that was seen by the victim, the approach would constitute assault and the impact would constitute battery. The victim, accordingly, would be entitled to damages both for the fear he felt from the threatened blow (assault) as well as the pain from the blow itself (battery).

Awareness of the Threat is Essential

A victim must be aware of a threat to be placed in apprehension of it. Thus an unconscious person cannot have a claim for assault but may have a claim for battery when he regains consciousness. If a victim is rendered unconscious by the first blow and is then kicked, he will have an action only for battery on the basis of the kick, which he never saw. The victim will have an action for both assault and battery for the first blow, which rendered him unconscious.

Reckless Misconduct

Although assault and battery are the main civil liabilities confronting the martial artist, he may also be held responsible for "reckless misconduct," even if another person has consented to practice with him. Although the law, in an attempt to create a "margin of safety" for those who choose to participate in socially beneficial sporting activities, permits a person to consent to purely negligent conduct, when an attacker's actions extend beyond the zone of negligence into the realm of recklessness, the law imposes liability upon the attacker. The distinctions between reckless misconduct and negligent misconduct, which in reality may be very obscure, are illustrated in the following discussion.

In the 1979 case of Jackrabbit v. Cincinnati Bengals, Inc., 601 F.2d 516 (10th Cir.), cert. denied, 444 U.S. 931 (1979), a defensive back for the Denver

Broncos, Dale "Jackrabbit" Hackbart, sued the Bengals and their offensive back, Charles "Booby" Clark, for an injury received during a professional football game. After Hackbart's teammate intercepted a pass intended for Clark, Hackbart attempted to block Clark by throwing his body in front of him. Hackbart remained kneeling on one knee watching his teammate return the intercepted pass to midfield when Clark, out of frustration, intentionally delivered a blow with his elbow to the back of Hackbart's head.

In the lawsuit that followed, the trial court dismissed the claim of assault and battery because the contact occurred during a sanctioned football game in which violence is condoned under the rules of the game as administered by football referees and officials. This view, however, was not followed by the court's appeal, which held that such reckless misconduct should not be permitted under the law.

Instead of relying on the common law theories of liability under the definition of assault and battery, the United States Tenth Circuit Court of Appeals, applying Colorado law, relied on Section 500 of the Restatement of Torts (2nd), which holds that a person should be liable when his misconduct is more than negligent and causes injury to another. Section 500 states in pertinent part as follows:

§ 500. Reckless Disregard of Safety Defined

The actor's conduct is in reckless disregard of the safety of another if he does an act . . . knowing or having reason to know of facts which would lead a reasonable man to realize, not only that his conduct creates an unreasonable risk of physical harm to another, but also that such risk is substantially greater than that which is necessary to make his conduct negligent.

By this definition of reckless misconduct, the objective standard of the "reasonable man" is applied to the conduct in question. The jury will be asked to apply this hypothetical measurement to the conduct based upon the evidence presented at trial, if the conduct is purely negligent, the defendant will not be found liable.

Thus, in jurisdictions such as Colorado that apply Section 500, even though a person has consented to be touched by virtue of his participation in a contact sport, the participants will not be immune from civil liability if they act recklessly toward one another and realize that such acts could cause a substantial risk of physical harm that is not merely negligent.

Reckless Versus Negligent Misconduct

Reckless misconduct is a greater wrong than negligent misconduct. Negligence implies unskillfulness or incompetence in one's actions, when compared to a reasonable standard of conduct, that causes risk of harm to another person. On the other hand, recklessness involves a conscious course of action by the wrongdoer that a reasonable person should recognize as involving risk of harm to others that is substantially greater than the risk involved from purely negligent actions. This consciousness that a substantial risk is created by a person's conduct makes a person's liability much greater in the eyes of the law. We will return to this concept of conscious wrongdoing in discussing potential criminal liability.

Negligent Misconduct

Negligence according to the law is not measured by the specific intent of a defendant to cause harm to a plaintiff. Rather, general rules are formulated

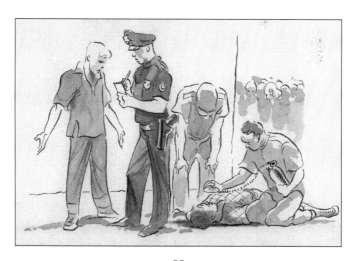

55

by the courts based on the duties that people owe to one another in society. The standard of care that a person must adhere to is the "reasonable man standard" under the circumstances involved. When a person breaches that duty, he will be liable for all damages that are proximately caused by his negligent actions.

Generally, negligent misconduct in the context of contact sports will not result in civil liability. This is illustrated in the case of Oswald v. Township High School Dist. No. 214, 406 N.E. 2d 157 (Ill. App. 1980). In this case, the plaintiff was injured when he was kicked while playing basketball in a required high school gym class. The plaintiff contended that the misconduct violated certain national high school safety rules for participants in basketball games. The Oswald court specifically held that negligence alone is not enough to impose liability upon a participant in a contact sport. To be held civilly liable, the court explained, the player's misconduct must be willful, wanton, or show "a reckless disregard" for the safety of the injured player. The court also approved a "margin of error" that permits the negligent violation of the rules of a game in the heat of the action. However, when a player's misconduct exceeds the negligent buffer zone and enters the realm of reckless disregard of the safety of others, then the reckless player will be held liable for any injuries he or she causes as a result of his or her reckless misconduct.

Assumption of Risk

Courts will apply the principle of "assumption of risk" in analyzing whether an instructor involved in karate training is negligently liable in causing injury to others while supervising his students. This concept was well explained in the New York case Beck v. Scimeca (Hwrang-Do Center), 90 N.Y.2d 471 (1997). The court explained that when a person engages in a sport or recreational activity, he consents to those commonly appreciated risks that are inherent in and arise out of the nature of the sport generally and that result from participation in the sport.

For example, the court observed that a person is legally deemed to accept responsibility for being hit by a ball in a baseball game or being bumped in a horse race. In each situation, the law will consider the degree of risk the plaintiff assumed when he elected to participate in the activity. The courts will not examine this in a vacuum. Their assessment is made against the background of the skill and experience of the participant.

In Scimeca, a 30-year-old orange belt student sued his instructor for compelling him to attempt a "jump roll" technique. In this case, a 15-year-old brown belt student took over the class and directed the older orange belt

student, who had been training for 15 months, to jump over a high barrier. Although the student had performed the technique before, the obstacle he had to jump over was raised higher than he had previously attempted and he sustained severe spinal injuries in his failed attempt.

The court held that the student had assumed the risk of attempting the new technique, which was calculated to advance his level of ability. The court examined whether the instructor had created dangerous conditions that were over and above the usual dangers inherent in the martial arts class. The court also made clear that to assume the risk the participant must not only have knowledge of the injury-causing activity but also an appreciation of the risk involved. Therefore, because the student had participated in this training technique before and appreciated the inherent risks, there was no negligence.

The court distinguished other cases involving sparring activities, which appear to place a higher degree of responsibility upon the instructor. For example, in Deangelis v. Izzo, 192 A.D.2d 823 (3d Dep't 1993), a beginning karate student sued the owner of his school after he sustained a serious head injury while sparring with another beginner. The court refused to dismiss the case based on assumption of risk. The court noted that karate is not a commonly observed activity such as baseball or football and that the dangers in karate are not as apparent as are the dangers in other common sports. Karate requires "specialized training" to make the punches, kicks, and blocks effective. In this case, the new students had been trained in the punches and kicks, but not in blocking them.

Interestingly, the court observed correctly that placing beginners together to spar may be more dangerous than having a beginner spar with a more experienced opponent. The court found that because this fact is counterintuitive, it was not clear that the risks involved were "known, apparent or reasonably foreseeable." Therefore, the court refused to dismiss the action and held it for trial.

Glossary

Assault: Threatening to strike or harm another person.

Assumption of risk: A defense to a claim for negligent injury to a person or property, i.e., a person who voluntarily exposes himself or his property to a known danger may not recover for injuries thereby sustained.

Battery: An unlawful touching, beating, wounding, or laying hold, however, trifling, of another's person or clothing without consent.

Defendant: One against whom a lawsuit is brought.

Mens rea: Criminal intent; evil intent; guilty intent.

Negligence: A flexible term for the failure to use ordinary care under the particular factual circumstances.

Plaintiff: One who initiates a lawsuit against another called the defendant.

Scienter: (knowingly, willfully), an element in crime and some civil wrongs, descriptive of the perpetrator's guilty knowledge.

Tort: Any one of various, legally recognized, private injuries or wrongs, which do not arise as the result of a breach of contract.

Endnotes

1   Prosser, W. (1981). *Handbook of the law of torts*, Section 2, at 7–9 (4th ed.) [hereinafter referred to as Prosser].

2   Prosser, Section 18, at 103.

3   Harper, F. & James, F. (1956). *The law of torts*, Section 3.10, at 233 [hereinafter referred to as Harper and James].

4   Draeger, D. & Smith, R. (1974). *Asian fighting arts*. Tokyo: Kodansha International, page 85.

5   Prosser, Section 19, at 110.

· 5 ·

Civil and Criminal Liability:
The Martial Artists Potential, Part II

by Noah Nunberg, J.D.

Illustrations courtesy of Oscar Ratti.
© 2001 Futuro Designs & Publications.

*Caution: The analysis and statements in this article are not meant as any form of legal advice. They are presented here merely for informative and educational purposes to assist the serious martial artist in understanding potential legal issues related to teaching, training, and self-defense. If you have a legal problem, please consult a qualified lawyer.

Introduction

Knowledge of assault and battery law is an aspect of martial arts training that has been sorely neglected. To understand how to react reasonably to an attack, the practitioner of any martial art should have a general understanding of society's code of conduct. Furthermore, society's standards are not shed at the door of the dojo with one's shoes. The law has crucial implications within the confines of the training hall. Although legal niceties do not strictly control a person's conduct during a street encounter or while training within a dojo, a martial artist should take time to reflect upon the legal consequences that may result from the use his techniques.

The present chapter focuses upon the criminal legal consequences that may arise from a non-fatal blow delivered by hand or foot to an assailant on the street or an opponent in practice. The distinction between criminal and civil law is fairly obvious. Criminal liability results from prosecution by the state for an offense or wrong committed against the public. The primary purpose of a criminal proceeding is to protect the public from an offender by punishing him or eliminating him from society.[1] Generally, the state, as protector of the public welfare, defines criminal offenses in statutes promulgated by the legislature. Civil liability, on the other hand, results from a civil proceeding brought, in the form of a lawsuit, by an individual (the plaintiff) seeking monetary compensation for damages resulting from a wrong or tort committed against him by another individual (the defendant). These two classes of liability are not mutually exclusive, that is, the same act can lead to both criminal and civil proceedings.

CRIMINAL LIABILITY

Criminal Versus Civil Liability

Most criminal statutes abandon the strict definition of the term "assault" and also use it when physical contact takes place. Before the criminal law aspects of using martial arts techniques are analyzed, the distinction between civil and criminal law should be reiterated. Civil law, by permitting courts to grant monetary or injunctive relief to a successful party, protects an individual's private rights from illegal interference by other individuals. In criminal law, something more than a private right is at stake: public consciousness and morality, as expressed in statutes, are being vindicated.

Further, as amplified below, a defendant must have *mens rea* (criminal intent) to be found guilty of a criminal act. A prosecutor must prove, beyond a reasonable doubt, not only the criminal act but also the degree of criminal intent that the defendant had when the crime was committed.

Consent Generally Cannot be Legally Given to a Criminal Act

This philosophy has practical implications. Whereas an individual may consent to being forcefully struck, thereby waiving his legal right to sue for the tort of battery committed against him, his consent cannot eliminate the crime that has been committed. In other words, individuals cannot with impunity consent to the commission of a crime. This is because the public's interest in safeguarding the health, safety, and welfare of its citizenry would otherwise be eroded by individuals who simply agree to break the law.[2] Accordingly, under

60

Section 35.15(1)(c) of New York Penal Law, a defendant cannot claim "self-defense" after he has engaged in "combat by agreement not specifically authorized by law."

Similarly, since the 19th century, dueling has been outlawed in all states, even if both parties consent to the activity, in recognition of society's interest in preventing the death or serious bodily harm of its citizenry. Dueling is defined as "the act of fighting with deadly weapons between two persons in pursuance of a previous agreement."[3] If both parties consent to the activity, the act is still criminal and they are still criminally liable.

The Defense of Consent

This is not to say that consent is totally irrelevant to the criminal law of assault and battery. In some instances when players were seriously injured in fights on the ice during hockey games, criminal prosecutions resulted. In a 1969 altercation involving Wayne Maki of the St. Louis Blues and Ted Green of the Boston Bruins, Green struck Maki in the face with his glove and stick. Maki retaliated by striking Green in the head with his stick, fracturing Green's skull. Green was charged with assault and Maki with aggravated assault. Both players were acquitted after their respective trials.

In the Green case, the court found that striking the face is a common occurrence in hockey and accordingly, that players consent to such foreseeable activity, at least when a high risk of serious injury is not involved. Maki on the other hand, was acquitted not because of any consent to the serious blows but because the court deemed his actions to be the instinctive reactions of self-defense. The Maki court discussed the consent defense but concluded that "there is a question of degree involved, and no athlete should be presumed to accept a malicious, unprovoked or overly violent attack."

More recently, NHL hockey player Marty McSorley, a Boston Bruins defenseman, was found guilty of assault with a weapon. As Donald Brashear, a Vancouver Canucks forward, skated with his back to McSorley, McSorley slashed him from behind with his stick and struck the side of his head. The court rejected McSorley's defense that NHL players give "explicit consent" to the risk of on-ice contact and that the blows therefore did not constitute an assault. It is therefore clear that a martial artist will not be immune from criminal prosecution if his conduct in the dojo is egregiously improper.

Consent to Bodily Harm

The 1962 proposed draft of the Model Penal Code attempted to formulate the defense of consent to bodily harm in the following language:

(2) Consent to Bodily Harm. When conduct is charged to constitute an offense because it causes or threatens bodily harm, consent to such conduct or to the infliction of such harm is a defense if:

(a) the bodily harm consented to or threatened by the conduct consented to is not serious; or

(b) the conduct and the harm are reasonably foreseeable hazards of joint participation in a lawful athletic or competitive sport....

Under this formulation, consent may be effective either when no serious injury is threatened by the activity or when both the conduct and the harm consented to are reasonably foreseeable within the activity itself.

The Role of Intent Under Criminal Law

To understand the criminal law of assault and battery, some basic concepts inherent in criminal law must be examined. Generally speaking, a crime is composed of two elements: (1) the commission of an illegal act and (2) the intent to do the act. Intent is technically referred to as *mens rea* ("guilty mind"). Therefore, the same act can have different legal consequences, depending on the intent with which it is committed. For example, if a defendant intends to wound his victim by shooting him with a gun but the victim is killed, the defendant is guilty of manslaughter. However, if the defendant shoots with the intent to kill his victim and accomplishes his desire, he has committed murder.

Degrees of Intent

The spectrum of intent, sometimes referred to as scienter, ranges upward as follows: "criminal negligence" ▶ "recklessness" ▶ "general intent" ▶ "specific intent." Criminal negligence, or gross negligence, is one degree above negligence, which, as explained in the previous chapter, is an objective standard used in tort law.

The negligence standard posits a hypothetically reasonable man acting, under the circumstances of a particular case, with the degree of care society deems to be reasonable. If the defendant acted unreasonably and created a foreseeable risk of harm to the defendant and as a direct consequence of the act, the plaintiff was injured, the negligent defendant will be held civilly liable for damages. However, negligence alone is insufficient to justify criminal prosecution.

Generally, proof of intent requires a prosecutor to show that a specific subjective evil motive was held by the perpetrator at the time he committed a crime. Proving that a defendant is civilly liable for negligence, in contrast, merely requires a demonstration of the objective unreasonableness of an act causing injury. The intent, or mens rea requirement for criminal conviction ranges from the very general and unformed (yet manifesting more guilt than mere negligence) to very specific intent to commit a particular act.

Let us use as an example a rude individual who, while walking down a sidewalk, suddenly sees another person in his way and instinctively pushes him aside to get past him. The rude individual has committed civil battery. However, if the rude individual were to punch his victim with the intent of striking his eye, a criminal act, not a tort, has been committed. In the latter example, the intent being motivated by a desire to cause physical injury, is more formulated and of a more evil nature in the eyes of the law than was the former instinctive act. The former example, in all probability, would not be considered a criminal act because of the lack of criminal intent. Nevertheless, the volitional act of touching another person was committed and a tort was thereby consummated.

Simple Versus Aggravated Assault

Historically in common law, all assaults and batteries were classified as simple assaults and treated as misdemeanors. Aggravated assault, a classification created by legislatures, required that a specific felonious intent be coupled with the act. The punishment meted out for aggravated assault was more severe than that for simple assault but less harsh than that for crime of mayhem, a common-law felony in which permanent injury was inflicted on a victim. Thus aggravated assault was a statutory bridge crossing the large common-law gap between simple assault and mayhem.[4]

Statutory Degrees of Assault

This historical, common-law distinction has been carried forward into contemporary criminal statutes. New York Penal Law has three degrees of assault. Assault in the third degree, a misdemeanor and the lowest degree of criminal assault, is defined as follows:

> Section 120.00 Assault in the third degree.
> A person is guilty of assault in the third degree when:
> (1) With the intent to cause physical injury to another person, he causes such injury to such person or to a third person; or
> (2) He recklessly causes physical injury to another person; or
> (3) With criminal negligence, he causes physical injury to another person by means of a deadly weapon or a dangerous instrument.

To cause "physical injury," as opposed to "serious bodily injury," is the action banned by the statute. The requisite mens rea, or evil intent, can range from the specific intent to cause physical injury (subparagraph 1) to recklessness, which is a less specific intent (subparagraph 2), to criminal negligence, which is the least blameworthy degree of intent but which requires the instrumentality of a deadly or dangerous instrument (subparagraph 3).

Assault in the second degree, a felony under Section 120.05 of the New York Penal Code, is a more serious crime in that the perpetrator must have intended to cause "serious physical injury to a person" and to have been successful in causing such injury either to the intended victim or another person. Alternatively, the statute defines second-degree assault as the intent to cause "physical injury" to another person and successfully causing such injury with a deadly weapon or dangerous instrument. The statute also defines second degree assault as the reckless infliction of serious injury with a deadly weapon or dangerous instrument.

Under Section 120.10 of New York Penal Law, first-degree assault follows the same pattern as do the other degrees. This section requires intent to cause "serious physical injury" and that such injury actually be caused "by means of a deadly weapon or a dangerous instrument." The next subsection, which resembles common-law mayhem, requires the specific intent "to disfigure another person seriously and permanently, or to destroy, amputate or disable permanently a member or organ" of another person's body and the actual

infliction such injury to the other person. It should be noted that the instrument used is irrelevant in this subsection. Accordingly, if an assailant intends to disfigure a victim or destroy an organ, such as an eye, and does so with an empty hand or unclad foot, he is guilty of first-degree assault.

It should also be noted that the statute does not require that the person against whom the defendant focuses his intent be the same person to whom the injury is inflicted. This concept is referred to as "transferred intent." Therefore, if person A intends to assault person B but instead accidentally assaults person C, the statutory requirements are satisfied even though the intended victim was not touched. The same concept exists in civil-law battery.

Case law fleshes out the above statutory definitions and makes them much more understandable. In People v. Hall, 209 N.Y.S.2d 917 (2d Dep't 1961), the defendant kicked his victim in the abdomen with such force as to rupture his liver, causing his death. The defendant's conviction under second-degree assault was reversed by the appellate court. Although the defendant had inflicted "grievous bodily harm," the court stated that it found no evidence to prove "the coextensive intent to inflict any 'grievous bodily harm' in defendant." Because there was a lack of proof of this essential element of specific intent, the second-degree assault conviction could not stand.

It should be noted that other jurisdictions do not accept this interpretation, saying instead that the intent to engage in the act of kicking would have sufficed for second-degree assault as long as the resulting injury was serious bodily injury or grievous bodily harm.

The Hand or Foot as a "Deadly Weapon"

Most important to the martial artist's analysis of the law is the question of whether the hand or foot can be classified as a deadly weapon or dangerous

instrument. As in many other areas of the law, there is no unity of opinion. Some jurisdictions accept a literal translation of the statute and hold that hands and feet are not commonly understood to be deadly weapons or dangerous instruments; therefore, assault with the hand or foot is not deemed to be aggravated assault with a deadly weapon or dangerous instrument. Other jurisdictions, including New York, have a broader view and hold that although feet and hands are not deadly or dangerous weapons per se, the manner of their use in particular situations may make them deadly weapons.[5]

New York Penal Law, Section 10.00, defines "deadly weapon" and "dangerous instrument," respectively, as follows:

(12) Deadly instrument means any loaded weapon from which a shot, readily capable of producing death or other serious physical injury, may be discharged, or a switchblade knife, gravity knife, dagger, billy, blackjack, or metal knuckles.

(13) Dangerous instrument means *any instrument, article or substance* [emphasis supplied], including a vehicle as that term is defined in this section, which, under the circumstances in which it is used, attempted to be used or threatened to be used, is readily capable of causing death or other serious physical injury.

The New York case of People v. Rumaner, 357 N.Y.S.2d 735 (3d Dep't 1974), discussed this particular question. A bouncer in a bar was grabbed by the defendant, who knocked him down and kicked him ten or twelve times in the face while wearing heavy boots. The victim was severely injured and his vision was permanently impaired. The defendant was convicted of second-degree assault.

The defendant argued on appeal that no intent had been proved, but this was rejected by the court. It held that the requisite intent could be inferred from the defendant's conduct. The fact that he stomped on the victim's head ten or twelve times negated any defense that his actions were inadvertent and provided sufficient proof of the required criminal intent.

The defendant also argued that his boots were not dangerous instruments, which was also rebuffed by the court, which stated:

> Any instrument, article or substance which under the circumstances in which it is used, is capable of causing death or other serious physical injury is a dangerous instrument within the meaning of the statute.

Therefore, the court concluded that the trier of fact was justified in finding that the boots were a dangerous instrument because they were used to inflict serious physical injury upon a victim.

In People v. Carter, 53 N.Y.2d 113 (1981), the New York Court of Appeals upheld a conviction of assault in the first degree in a case where the defendant, while wearing rubber boots, punched and kicked his victim into a comatose state. The Court held that the rubber boots were "dangerous instruments" in light of the manner in which the defendant administered the "vicious stomping." The Court noted that the New York definition of dangerous instrument is expansive enough to make any object, no matter how innocuous it may be when used for its normal purpose, a dangerous instrument "when it is used in a manner which renders it readily capable of causing serious physical injury." Even a handkerchief, the court noted, can fall into this definition when used to asphyxiate a victim, although it is by no means an inherently dangerous instrument.

Although many cases look to the type of shoe or boot worn by the defendant to see if a dangerous instrument was in fact used, jurisdictions in which courts apply an expanded interpretation of "deadly weapon" or "dangerous instrument" may hold that an unclad foot or fist falls within these categories.

Certainly these courts will look to the circumstances in which they are used, including the ability and strength with which the perpetrator uses them. A prosecutor therefore could, and most certainly would, use the fact that a person is highly trained in a martial art to show that his use of his hands or feet constitute the use of a deadly weapon or dangerous instrument, when serious bodily injury is ultimately inflicted by the martial artist.

The "Self-Defense" Defense

A properly trained martial artist will have, in most instances, the defense of self-defense. Under New York Penal Law, self-defense is known as the defense of "justification," as defined under Section 35.15. The statute classifies this defense into two major categories: either simple physical force or deadly physical force used to defend oneself or another person. With regard to the use of physical force, this section provides as follows:

> Section 35.15 Justification; use of physical force in defense of a person
>
> (1) A person may, subject to the provisions of subdivision two, use physical force upon another person when and to the extent he reasonably believes such to be necessary to defend himself or a third person from what he reasonably believes to be the use or imminent use of unlawful physical force by such other person, unless:
>
> (a) The latter's conduct was provoked by the actor himself with intent to cause physical injury to another person; or
>
> (b) is nevertheless justifiable if he has withdrawn from the encounter and effectively communicated such withdrawal to such other person but the latter persists in continuing the incident by the use or threatened imminent use of unlawful physical force:
>
> (c) The physical force involved is the product of a combat by agreement not specifically authorized by law.

As previously noted, force may be used to defend oneself or another person when there is a reasonable belief that an attack of like nature is being made upon the defender or another person, even though this reasonable belief may in reality be a mistaken one.

Furthermore, if the initial aggressor effectively withdraws, he may defend himself against any uncalled for onslaught by the initial victim. Thus the law only recognizes self-defense when an attack is in progress or is imminent; it does not allow the victim to pursue a course of revenge against his assailant after the attack is over.

With regard to "deadly physical force," Section 35.15 provides as follows:

(2) A person may not use deadly physical force upon another person under the circumstances specified in subdivision one unless

  (a) He reasonably believes that such other person is using or is about to use deadly physical force. Even in such a case, however the actor may not use deadly physical force if he knows that he can with complete safety as to himself and others avoid the necessity of so doing by retreating, except he is under no duty to retreat if he is:

    (i) in his dwelling and not the initial aggressor; or

    (ii) a police officer or peace officer or a person assisting a police officer or peace officer at the latter's direction, acting pursuant to section 35.330; or

  (b) He reasonably believes that such other person is committing or attempting to commit a kidnaping, forcible rape, forcible sodomy or robbery; or

  (c) He reasonably believes that such other person is committing or attempting to commit a burglary, and the circumstances are such that the use of deadly physical force is authorized by subdivision three of Section 35.20.

This section makes clear that deadly force may be used when like force is being used or is about to be used against a victim; however, there is a clear duty to retreat when this may be done safely. The duty to retreat does not apply when a person is in his home and is not the initial aggressor. Also, a police officer does not need to retreat when he is making a felony arrest, a circumstance that usually includes a crime involving the use or threatened use of physical force. Furthermore, an individual who is rightfully in a dwelling or an occupied building may use deadly force if (1) he reasonably believes a burglary is being committed or attempted and (2) he reasonably believes such force to be necessary to prevent the commission or attempted commission of the burglary.

As can be seen, the law is quite exacting in its requirements before permitting an individual to use deadly physical force to protect himself. However, when a martial artist uses his empty hands or bare feet to defend himself, the law rarely finds such force to be deadly. Certainly if the attacker is rendered unconscious by the martial artist's blows, the defender must, under the law, stop his defensive attack because the initial aggressor has been rendered helpless. If the defensive attack is continued, the martial artist becomes the aggressor and becomes criminally liable for his actions.

Within the dojo, criminal violations may occur if practitioners engage in conflict that escalates beyond the reasonable realm of normal practice and the participants intend to inflict serious physical harm upon each other and are successful in doing so. As the cases noted above make clear, kicking a victim with intent to cause serious injury constitutes criminal assault when such injury is actually inflicted.

Let us examine, as we did in the companion chapter, a hypothetical situation wherein person A blocks person B's incoming knife attack during a practice session in the dojo. Person B stands still and allows person A to complete his defensive maneuvers. A, who has lost many free-style matches to B, now sees an opportunity to eliminate his foe and kicks B violently in the pubic region, causing severe internal hemorrhaging. Under these circum- stances, A is guilty of second-degree assault because he intended to cause serious physical injury to B and was successful in doing so. The fact that B consented to practice knife attacks with A is no legal defense for A's criminal act because, when A embarked on his course of revenge, his actions clearly exceeded the bounds of B's consent.

If, however, B perceives A's violent attack and instinctively protects himself with a technique that causes serious injury to A, B then will have the legal defense of justification. B reasonably believed that A departed from the training or exercise that they agreed to engage in and that A was attempting to cause him physical harm. Under such circumstances, B could use reasonable force to defend himself from the physical attack but could not, however, use the knife to stab A in the chest. Deadly physical force was not threatened by A; B therefore cannot use such force on A.

Conclusion

As can be seen from the above discussion, students of the martial arts must take into account the law of assault and battery when they use martial techniques both inside and outside of the dojo. Serious students of the martial arts who reasonably employ their techniques solely for defensive purposes on

70

the street and who comport with the "warriors' ethical code" (*bushido*) within the dojo probably should have no legal problems as a result of using their training. But a student who misuses the weaponless weapon his instructor has given him will not do so with legal impunity.

Glossary

Assault: Threatening to strike or harm another person.

Assumption of risk: A defense to a claim for negligent injury to a person or property, i.e., a person who voluntarily exposes himself or his property to a known danger may not recover for injuries thereby sustained.

Battery: An unlawful touching, beating, wounding, or laying hold, however, trifling, of another's person or clothing without consent.

Defendant: One against whom a lawsuit is brought.

Mens rea: Criminal intent; evil intent; guilty intent.

Negligence: A flexible term for the failure to use ordinary care under the particular factual circumstances.

Plaintiff: One who initiates a lawsuit against another called the defendant.

Scienter: (knowingly, wilfully), an element in crime and some civil wrongs, descriptive of the perpetrator's guilty knowledge.

Tort: Any one of various, legally recognized, private injuries or wrongs, which do not arise as the result of a breach of contract.

Endnotes

[1] Prosser, W. (1981). *Handbook of the law of torts* (4th ed.). Section 19, at 110.

[2] Note. Consent in criminal law: Violence in sports. *Michigan Law Review*, 75, 148, 150 n. 12, 162–163. 1976.

[3] 28 Corp. Jur. Sec., Dueling Section 1, at 580. 1941.

[4] *Model Penal Code and Commentaries*, Part II, Section 211.11, Comment 1(a). 1980.

[5] Annot. (1970). *Kicking as aggravated assault, or assault with dangerous or deadly weapon*, 33 A.L.R.3d 922.

· 6 ·

Comprehensive Penitentiary Defense as Developed for Use in Spain

by F. Rodríguez Román, Ph.D. and C. Gutiérrez García, Ph.D.

All photographs courtesy of Francisco Javier Rodríguez Román.

"To injure an opponent is to injure yourself.
To control aggression without inflicting
injury is the Art of Peace"
~ Morihei Ueshiba, founder of aikido

Introduction

Prisons constitute a unique working environment, set apart from all others by the combination of features peculiar to the context in which the prison professionals operate. The responsibilities of the latter include ensuring the safety of inmates and enforcing prison rules, while at the same time taking an active role in the process of social reintegration of prisoners. Many of those who work in the prison system—prison officers, medical personnel, teachers, social workers, psychologists, members of the legal profession, volunteers, etc.—come into direct contact with the inmate population. The past criminal activities of inmates and coexistence within the prison often emerge as sources of tension that may lead to various manifestations of conflict affecting any person forming part of prison society. For example, in answer to the question posed by the independent MP, Carlos Casimiro Salvador Armendáriz, on April 17, 2008, concerning aggressions committed by inmates against prison personnel between March 2004 and March 2008, the Spanish government supplied the following figures (BOCG, 2008): 1 extremely serious aggression and 11 serious aggressions in 7 centers in 2004 (from March); 1 extremely serious aggression and 9 serious aggressions in 9 centers in 2005; 32 serious aggressions in 21 centers in 2006; 15 serious aggressions in 14 centers in 2007; and 1 serious aggression in 1 center in 2008 (up to March).

In this environment, knowledge of self-defense techniques constitutes a valuable resource that could facilitate conflict resolution. Comprehensive Penitentiary Defense (CPD) is defined as a set of techniques aimed at achieving resolution of the conflicts that may arise in a prison environment, for example, preventing fights between prisoners, preventing self-harm, resolving active or passive resistance,[1] dealing with attacks on prison staff, overcoming armed subjects, handcuffing techniques, and using statutory defense[2] equipment and self-defense techniques. The physical aspects[2] of these techniques have their origins in the traditional martial arts such as karate, aikido, judo, kobudo, or kenjutsu, and are applied as required within the limits of correct use of coercive measures envisaged by the law. CPD represents an attempt to safeguard, through the selection and combination of the most appropriate techniques for each situation, the physical safety of both inmates and staff in the prison system.

Comprehensive Penitentiary Defense

With the aim of ensuring that prison inmates do not have access to arms (defined in the broadest terms as any instrument that could be used to defend oneself or to attack), prison legislation permits the use of body searches and inspections as the most suitable means—together with surveillance of inmates, roll calls, room searches, and controls—for ensuring prison security. Thus, Article 23 of the General Penitentiary Organic Law 1/1979, of the 26th September (LOGP) establishes that "Inspections and body searches of inmates, their belongings and the cells they occupy, roll-calls, together with inspection of prison facilities will be performed where necessary, with the guarantees and regularity established by the regulations and observing respect for personal dignity."

Likewise, Article 68.1 of Royal Decree 190/199, of the 9th February, approving Penitentiary Regulations (RP), states that "Body searches and examination of inmates' clothes and possessions, together with the inspection of doors, windows, floors, walls and ceilings in cells or bedrooms, and in communal areas, will be conducted."

Nevertheless, despite the rigorous application of all measures envisaged by the law on the part of prison staff, aimed at optimizing prison security, inmates frequently employ their time and imagination in constructing hand-made arms. The most well-known sharp instrument is that called a "shiv" or "shank," a very sharp, pointed instrument capable of producing severe injury. It can be made from a variety of objects, such as a section of a broom or mop handle, a shard of glass with a bandage or some plastic for the handle, a filed toothbrush handle hardened over a flame, a latch, the flashing or frame of a window, or the metal mounting of a fluorescent light shaped like a dagger. Therefore, although the majority of attacks by inmates on staff are carried out with their bare hands, the appearance of a weapon as dangerous as the blade mentioned above can significantly increase the danger of any conflict.

Left: Various hand-made shivs confiscated from inmates. **Right:** An excellent wooden imitation of a pistol, shown next to a genuine pistol.

As mentioned above, prison staff can be the target of inmate aggressions. It should be noted that prison officers, that is, those in direct contact with the inmates, do not carry any kind of statutory weapon. As established in Article 45 of the LOGP, a prison officer may not habitually carry a firearm nor coercive instruments such as statutory defense equipment or handcuffs, as these are reserved exclusively for situations of disruption to prison order. All coercive instruments available to the prison officer must be secured in an appropriate place: point 4 of Article 72, RP: "Physical coercive implements shall be deposited in such a place or places as the Governor considers appropriate..."

As a result of these regulations, prison officers frequently have no other recourse than their strength and physical expertise when dealing with conflict that requires the use of physical self-defense techniques.

The proportionality of the techniques employed by a prison officer is fundamental to the re-establishment of normality following a disruption of order. Once dialogue, the first line of conflict resolution, has been exhausted, the prison officer must employ the most appropriate technique for the circumstances, according to the level of resistance proffered. The technique chosen should be that which will enable the officer to take control of the situation while causing as little harm as possible to the ringleader or leaders of the disruption.

Accordingly, the ideas and founding principles of CPD are to transmit in a practical and real way that the basic precept in any situation of risk or conflict, whether involving inmates or staff, is to "stop and/or avoid conflict":

- Because inmates express clear aggression or violence, or repeatedly and continually persist in disrupting normal life in the prison.
- When there is no other, less drastic means of stopping or avoiding conflict.
- Until normality is restored.
- Strictly for the duration necessary.

The keys to stopping or avoiding conflict should be:

- First, to possess sufficient autonomy and self-determination in order to tackle the conflict with proportionality and appropriate measures (the principle of minimum intervention).
- Second, to develop the capacity and skills necessary to tackle conflict within the bounds of the regulations and in the least damaging and harmful way possible.

The aim of CPD is to teach prison staff, particularly those in direct contact with inmates, how to use self-defense techniques (both physical and otherwise) in a proportionate and appropriate way, achieving maximum effect with minimum possible intervention. Indeed, the principle of minimum intervention should be the guiding precept behind all actions undertaken by prison staff. Thus, the fundamental aim of prison systems should be to maintain a climate conducive to the successful outcome of the treatment received by inmates, where prison rules are seen as the means to this end rather than an end in themselves. Without underestimating the security aspect of prisons, the underlying philosophy to this approach is that the first priority of a prison is to provide treatment for the inmates. The aim of such treatment is the social reintegration of the subject currently deprived of his or her liberty. Prison organization, which strives to achieve optimum coexistence among inmates, should never constitute a hindrance to the implementation of such treatment.

- **Comprehensive:** This system of self-defense comprises both physical and non-physical self-defense techniques. The physical techniques comprise a selection of different martial arts techniques, and thus constitute both a global and utilitarian approach to the martial arts, and a specific approach when selecting the most appropriate technique to employ in order to resolve a variety of situations.
- **Penitentiary:** Situations of disruption unique to the prison environment require rapid, efficient, and proportionate resolution. The solutions applicable in other, more general systems are usually insufficient or inappropriate, as they are not framed within the context of prison reality.
- **Defense:** The prison officer should always seek to avoid conflict through the use of the least harmful techniques possible in order to achieve successful resolution of situations where order has been disrupted.

Legal Framework

With the aim of elucidating the regulatory framework for intervention on the part of prison staff as regards the use of coercive measures, the basic legal aspects concerning such use, detailed in Article 45 of the LOGP and Article 72 of the RP, are outlined below.

The use of coercive measures are considered appropriate in the case of avoiding attempts to abscond, preventing inmates from inflicting self-harm or from harming others, and overcoming active or passive resistance on the part of inmates to prison staff orders. When the use of coercive measures is deemed necessary, a protocol must be followed consisting in communicating this need to the prison governor in order to obtain authorization. The latter is responsible for informing the parole board. In cases of extreme urgency, the most appropriate coercive measure may be applied, and the governor informed immediately afterward; the governor in turn, informs the parole board. Coercive measures envisaged under the law include temporary isolation, personal physical force, rubber truncheons, appropriate aerosol sprays and handcuffs. Under no circumstances is the use of firearms permitted. Instruments of coercion are kept in the place or places the governor considers most appropriate, and thus a prison officer never carries any coercive measure except his or her own physical strength. Given that the exclusive aim of the use of coercive measures is to re-establish normality, they can only be used in the case of disruption to order. Where such disruptions are serious, involving imminent danger to people or facilities, prison security forces may impose order provisionally when requested to do so by the governor.

Finally, the application of coercive measures is not envisaged in certain circumstances: with pregnant women, with women up to six months after giving birth, with nursing mothers, and with women accompanied by their children. Neither can they be applied with patients recovering from serious illness, except where this would avoid imminent danger to them or others.

TECHNICAL SECTION

As a preventative measure within the prison context, it is necessary to maintain appropriate body posture. This position enables us to intervene at any time. In this posture the weight of the body is evenly distributed on both legs, with the feet held a shoulder's width apart. One foot should be further forward than the other, forming a 45 degree angle, and the weight of the body should fall more on the ball of the foot than on the heel.

Likewise, an appropriate safety distance from the interlocutor should be maintained. Maintaining this distance has a double aim: on the one hand, it enables us to avoid a possible attack, providing time to react rapidly due to the response time afforded by the distance from the attacker; and on the other hand, this distance enables us to maintain visual contact with the other inmates, as the attacker does not occupy the majority of our field of vision.

The normal safety distance is defined as the equivalent of an arm-and-a-half's length, and corresponds to a normal situation—for example, a conversation between a prison officer and an inmate. At this distance, an inmate could reach the prison officer with a kick, or a fist if this attack is accompanied by movement. Careful observation of body language and the inmate's attitude (gesture, body posture, and look) will enable a prison officer to foresee the start of an attack. In this new situation, the officer will adopt the emergency safety distance, equivalent to a leg-and-a-half's length. From this distance, the officer can tackle and fend off any type of attack more easily.

Left:
Appropriate body posture.
This body posture enables a rapid response to any unexpected situation.

Right:
Response to an unexpected attack.
Faced with an imminent attack by an inmate, an appropriate posture will enable the prison officer to effect an indirect attack on the inmate's face.

As this is a prison context—clearly very different from a martial arts sports competition, or even a street fight—the officer will maintain a conciliatory attitude toward the inmate, sustaining a dialogue, reprimanding the inmate if necessary, or writing up reports on inmate behavior, whether positive (good behavior report) or negative (incident report), all in an atmosphere of normality. If the officer sees that the inmate moves from a calm attitude to one of violence, his or her first recourse will be to maintain eye contact, indicate agreement through gesture, and use appropriate language to redirect the violent attitude toward calmness. All this should be done without conspicuously adopting a defensive physical posture, such as raised arms, which would be to invite combat. If the inmate maintains an aggressive attitude, he or she should be subdued using the minimum physical force necessary, or, if there is a risk that this disturbance could extend further—for example, in the case of a group of inmates in a common area such as the prison yard or dining room—the officer should adopt the emergency safety distance and notify the senior officer immediately. The senior officer should then mobilize the support necessary to isolate and resolve the incident as rapidly and proportionately as possible.

SITUATIONS & AND PROCEDURES
illustrated on the following pages

- Body Searches
- Entering a Cell
- Aggression among Inmates
- Prisoner Transfer
- Techniques against Grips
- Active Resistance
- Use of Handcuffs
- Statutory Defense Equipment
- Techniques against Unarmed Attacks
- Techniques against Attacks with Sharpened Weapons

Body Searches

The prison officer has two methods at his or her disposal for conducting body searches on inmates: a metal detector and physical examination. The use of a metal detector is indicated in order to find sharp objects or "shivs" (home-made blades). Physical examination is useful for confiscating both blades and drugs. Frequently, and especially after a fight between inmates, both methods are employed in unison, since the opponents may be carrying some kind of weapon, such as a stone inside a sock or knotted t-shirt for use as a sling, or a shiv made of a material that is not detected by a metal detector (plastic, bone, glass).

Should the inmate offer passive resistance during the body search, the prison officer will effect control of the inmate's upper or lower body, or both. Finally, control from behind is achieved by bending the inmate's wrist.

(a) Control of the upper body for body searches: To control the upper body, we shift our weight forward by flexing the forward knee, and position our forearm down the inmate's spine. This prevents the inmate from hitting us with his or her elbow.

(b) Control of the lower body for body searches: To attain control of the lower body, we shift our weight forward, pushing our knee against the inmate's popliteal fossa (back of the knee). This prevents the inmate from kicking backwards.

(c) Control following a body search: We finish the intervention by achieving control from behind, pushing our left knee against the inmate's right popliteal fossa, and our left forearm down the inmate's spine. Our right hand holds the inmate's right thumb, lifting it to his or her shoulder.

(d) Control following a body search: Once the thumb is under control, we control the position of the wrist with our left hand. At the same time, with our right hand resting on the inmate's right shoulder, we help the inmate to regain normal posture from the previously unbalanced position he or she maintained against the wall.

(e) Body search variation: If the subject is taller than the officer, we change the position of our forward leg. In this case, the leg is held perpendicular to that of the inmate, with our foot resting on the inmate's instep and our forward arm resting above his or her elbow. For example, if we are searching the left side of the inmate, we control his or her left arm with our left hand and use our right hand to search the back of the inmate's body. Subsequently, we reverse positions. This new position enables us to search the entire length of the subject's arm without reducing prison-officer safety.

Entering a Cell

The inmate may display resistance in the cell, manifesting a violent attitude and even carrying one or more pointed instruments. The subject may use a throwing weapon or an irritant product. In order to hinder the work of the officers, the inmate may even have covered the cell floor with soapy water. Faced with this situation, officers should employ appropriate equipment when taking action (shield, helmet, jackets, truncheon, handcuffs), and take the precaution of carrying the truncheon with the leather loop around their wrists. This prevents the inmate from appropriating the truncheon, and also aids in subsequent control of the subject by bending his or her wrist.

Holding the truncheon (a): The truncheon is held firmly until the officer has removed the pointed instrument from the inmate.

Holding the truncheon (b): The truncheon is essential when the inmate is carrying a shiv.

PRISONER TRANSFER

In prisons, the transfer of inmates from one section of the building to another is a frequent occurrence (in order to participate in sporting or religious activities, to attend voluntary cultural activities, etc). Such transfers may also be from one section to another that the inmate does not like, for example, a change of section following participation in a fight.

Transfer

(a): If the inmate offers passive resistance during the transfer from one section to another in the building, we will offer the same, positioning ourselves by the inmate's side and controlling his or her elbow by holding it against our solar plexus.

(b): If the inmate raises an arm and clenches his or her fist in an attempt to increase resistance to control, we will exert pressure through friction and control of the wrist.

(c): The pressure exerted by the elbow on the inmate's side dictates the minimum distance between officer and inmate.

(d): If the inmate stands on tiptoe, this indicates that the technique has produced the desired effect of control, thus preventing the inmate from attacking the officer with his or her free hand.

ACTIVE RESISTANCE

When the inmate shows evident signs of agitation, and with the aim of avoiding potential aggression toward prison staff or other inmates, the inmate in question should be subdued with one of the following techniques and using the minimum force necessary.

The Lift

(a): Moving forward with our left leg, we take hold of the inmate's right wrist with our right hand. During this initial movement, we lift the inmate's hand up to his or her shoulder, with his or her elbow facing upward.

(b): Maintaining flexion of the wrist, we reinforce this with the help of our left hand. After raising the inmate's hand, and with his or her elbow joint blocked, we push the inmates arm out straight, toward the floor.

(c): Without changing the position of our left hand, we bend the inmate's arm with our right hand, pulling his or her elbow toward us while at the same time turning around to position ourselves behind the inmate.

(d): Maintaining the control achieved with the right hand, we secure wrist flexion with our left hand.

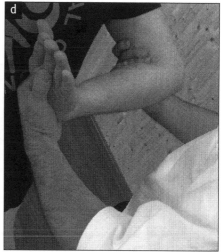

The Spider

This technique, when performed rapidly, unbalances and immobilizes the subject.

(a): We move forward on the left foot while pushing the inmate's chin upward with our right hand.

(b): As the inmate falls backward, we create a space between his or her arm and side. Positioning our left arm in this space, we pivot, changing our direction of movement. At the same time, we use our left forearm to apply pressure on the inmate's trapezius muscle until the inmate's body is in a horizontal position.

(c): Using our right hand, we secure the position of the left arm, and can begin to move forward.

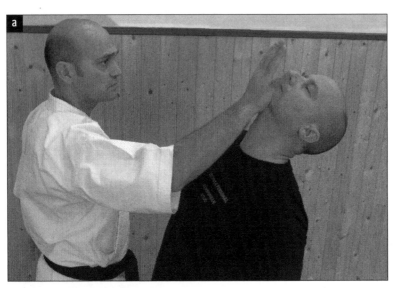

The Sickle

(a): We move forward on our left leg while pulling the inmate's body forward with our right arm.

(b): Changing direction, we pass our left arm between the inmate's arm and side. Maintaining pressure on his or her neck with our right arm, we form a right angle with both forearms.

Horizontal Walk

(a): We move forward on the left leg while gripping the inmate's right-hand wrist with our right hand. We immediately grasp the same with our left hand. Using the right hand, we bend the inmate's arm, pulling his or her elbow toward our body.

(b): Raising our left forearm to the height of the inmate's shoulder, we apply pressure until the inmate's body forms a horizontal line.

(c): With our right hand, we secure the position of our left forearm across the inmate's back, and can begin to move forward.

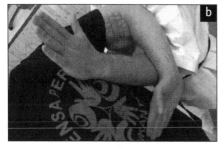 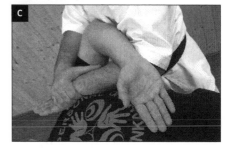

The Tray

(a): Starting from a position behind the inmate, we move forward on our left leg while gripping the inmate's arm. We then move forward on our right leg while using our right hand in a semicircular upward motion to raise the inmate's hand to the height of his or her shoulder.

(b): We use our left hand to secure the control achieved with our right hand.

AGGRESSION AMONG INMATES

Aggression between inmates requires the involvement of prison officers, who should apply the technique in unison. This technique consists of applying pressure with the knuckles of the index and middle fingers in the subject's lumbar zone, while at the same time applying pressure with the outer edge of the foot to the popliteal fossa (back of knee), and taking control of the neck from behind.

Inmates Fights

(a): We apply downward pressure on the inmate's lumbar zone with the knuckles of our left hand.

(b): We begin to turn our body, applying pressure with the outer edge of our foot on the back of the inmate's left knee, achieving increased imbalance.

(c): Using our right hand, we gain control from behind.

STATUTORY DEFENSE EQUIPMENT

The statutory defense equipment (a rubber truncheon) is 50 cm (19.7") long and 3 cm (1.2") thick. It is a semirigid weapon that can be used to effect immobilization, for example, containment of violent subjects, or for striking, for example, in the case of an inmate armed with a shiv.

Forward Control with the Statutory Defense Equipment

(a): Moving forward on the right leg, we position the truncheon between the inmate's left arm and body.

(b): Pivoting on the right foot, we grip the truncheon with our left hand.

(c): Positioning our hands on either side of the inmate's shoulder, we apply downward pressure.

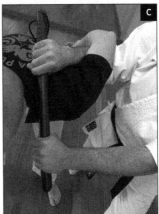

Control from Behind with the Statutory Defense Equipment

(a): Positioned behind the inmate, we move forward on our left leg and pass the truncheon downward, between the inmate's left arm and side.

(b): Gripping the truncheon under our right armpit, we make a semicircular movement with the right arm, pulling the inmate's left forearm upward.

(c): With our right forearm we push the inmate's left forearm upward, while with our left hand we pull the truncheon toward the left.

(d): We grasp the subject with our right hand, reinforcing the hold with our left hand and applying downward pressure with both hands.

USE OF HANDCUFFS

The Sleeping Cobra

(a): Moving forward on our left leg, we grip the inmate's right arm.

(b): Positioning our thumb in the unoccupied cuff, we pivot on our right foot.

(c): Once both hands have been cuffed, we grasp the center of the handcuffs, pulling them upward.

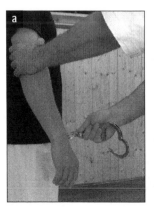

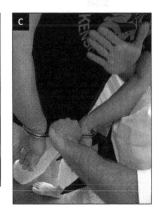

Handcuffing Especially Violent Inmates

(a): Holding the inmate's right arm with our left hand, we proceed to handcuff the subject.

(b): We pull the unoccupied cuff toward the floor with our right hand, in the direction in which the subject is moving.

(c): We then pull the handcuffs between the inmate's legs, changing our hold on the unoccupied ring from the right to the left hand.

(d): With both hands cuffed between the legs, an individual is considerably less dangerous.

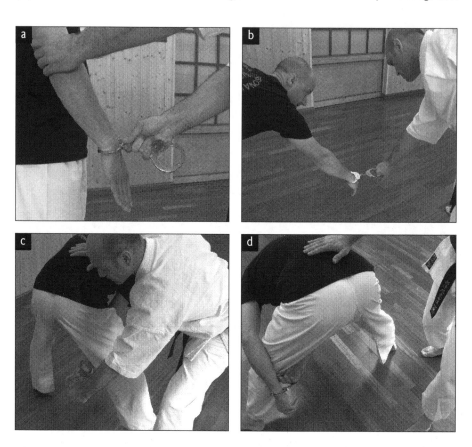

Techniques Against Grips

Should an inmate grip an officer by the lapels, the following solutions are given, among others:

Defense against a Lapel Grip

(a): While stepping backward, we join the inmate's wrists with a simultaneous horizontal push using both our hands.

(b): Moving forward on the left foot, we apply pressure with the index and middle fingers to the base of the inmate's trachea.

 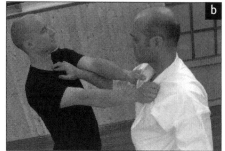

TECHNIQUES AGAINST UNARMED ATTACKS
Absorbing the attack, control on the floor, and transfer.

Defense Against Unarmed Attacks — I

(a): If the inmate throws a circular punch with his or her right arm, we block it with our left arm while gripping the inmate's neck with our right arm. Turning, we throw him or her to the ground.

(b): Securing a wrist block with our right hand, we move in a semicircular direction around his or her head.

(c): Once the inmate's arm is blocked, we control his or her wrist with our left hand.

(d): Passing the inmate's right hand under his or her armpit, we maintain control of his or her wrist and with a circular motion we raise the inmate.

(e): Once standing, we secure control of the inmate's wrist by raising his or her elbow.

  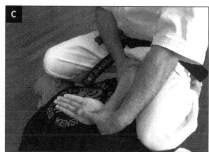

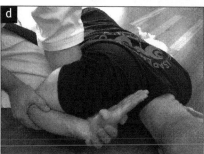 

Defense Against Unarmed Attacks — II

(a): Moving to the right of the inmate, we intercept the attacking arm with our right arm.

(b): Grasping the inmate's arm with our left hand, we move forward on our right leg toward the subject's back, controlling his or her right wrist.

(c): Once the inmate's arm and wrist are controlled we can begin to move forward.

TECHNIQUES AGAINST ARMED ATTACKS WITH SHARPENED WEAPONS

Defense Against Armed Attacks — I

(a): Moving away and toward the left, we intercept the upward attack with both hands.

(b): Moving both wrists vertically, we raise the inmate's arm.

(c): Raising the attacking hand, we turn to pass beneath the inmate's arm.

(d): We flex the inmate's wrist until he or she drops the weapon.

SIMULTANEOUS HALT AND STRIKE WITH CONTROL OF THE ELBOW

Defense Against Armed Attacks — II

(a): We block the inmate's attack with our left forearm.

(b): We grasp the inmate's wrist with both hands.

(c): We turn to the right, moving forward on the left leg.

(d): We keep our left arm beneath the attacking arm.

(e): Once the attacker's arm is positioned over our shoulder, we flex his or her elbow until the inmate drops the weapon.

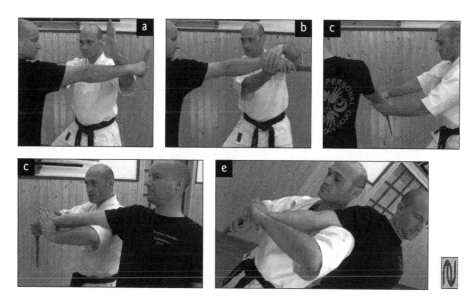

Notes

[1] Active resistance is defined as a violent refusal on the part of the inmate to comply with orders received from prison officers in the legitimate exercise of their duties, for example, the inmate refuses to enter a prison section. Passive resistance is defined as the refusal to obey prison officers' orders in the execution of their duties, which leads to disruption of the order, for example, the inmate does not wish to attend trial and refuses to leave his or her cell.

[2] Social skills, such as active listening, empathy, self-control, formulation of questions, reinforcement, or feedback also form part of comprehensive penitentiary defense, and their correct use can resolve conflict without recourse to physical intervention. Nonetheless, in this article the author focuses solely on the physical aspects of comprehensive penitentiary defense.

Bibliography

Koga, R. and Pelkey, W. (1995). *Controlling force: A primer for law enforcement* (second edition). Fallbrook, CA: The Koga Institute.

Koga, R. and Pelkey, W. (1998). *Redirecting force: A manual of law enforcement. Self-defense.* Fallbrook, CA: The Koga Institute.

Ley Oragànci (1/1979, de 26 de Septiembre), General Penitenciaria.

Official Bulletin (2008, November 20). Answer to the question posed by Mr. Carlos Casimiro Salvador Armendáriz (GP) concerning aggressions committed by inmates against prison personnel between March 2004 and March

2008. B.O.C.G. [Official Bulletin of the Spanish Congress of Deputies], series D, (109): 399-400.

Quiròs Martìnez, J. (2002). *Karate-do: Posiciones, desplazamientos y defensas. Tomo I.* Madrid: Asociación de la Prensa Hispanoamericana.

Quiròs Martìnez, J. (2007). *Tsuki waza: Ataques directos. Tomo II.* Madrid: Zanshin Karate-do.

Real Decreto (190/1996, de 9 de febrero), por el que se aprueba el Reglamento Penitenciario.

Rodrìguez Romàn, F. (2007). *Defensa personal y utilización correcta de medios coercitivos* [DVD]. Badajoz: Autor-Editor.

Sugawara, T. and Lujian, X. (1996). *Aikido and Chinese martial arts: Its fundamental relations. Volume 1.* Tokyo: Sugawara Martial Arts Institute.

Sugawara, T., Lujian, X. and Jones, M. (1998). *Aikido and weapons training. Volume 2.* Tokyo: Sugawara Martial Arts Institute.

Acknowledgements

The authors would like to express their gratitude to the following people, without whom it would not have been possible to write this article: Julio César Benito Luengo (participation as uke); Mario Jiménez García (photography), Francisco Javier Benito González (Home Office Official), and José Antonio Yuste Costa (Head of Prison Services, for providing prohibited objects); Carmelo Charfolé Hernández (Director of Badajoz Prison, for legal advice); Eva Alor Blasco (technical assistance); Translation Office of the University of León and Pedro Jorge Rodríguez Román (language assistance), the *ACAIP* (Administration of Penitentiary Institutions Group) *Journal* (www.acaip.info, contributing photographs and data); Tetsutaka Sugawara for being a source of inspiration (www.sugawarabudo.com); and Pedro Martín González and the Kenshinkan Dojo for their teaching (www.kenshinkandojo.badajoz.com). Correspondence to the authors can be sent to: romandip@hotmail.es.

· 7 ·

Using Gradual Force and Applying Techniques from the System of Comprehensive Penitentiary Defense

by Francisco J. Rodrìguez Romàn, B.A.

"What you get by force won't last long;
what you get by reason will last forever."
— Hironori Ohtsuka

The prison officer must know how to transform an inmate's violent attitude back to normality by means of resources such as active listening (paying attention to what the inmate means to communicate) in order to achieve the information needed to proactively solve a potential problem. On many an occasion, a simple conversation will be enough to keep an inmate from escalating aggressively, just because what they only need is to be heard. Another very useful technique is assertiveness, that is to say, getting to control the other party without pushing them around and without giving up our own interests. Body language techniques will be equally important: space (not invading the personal space, by keeping a proper distance for communication, while still within an normal safety distance [Rodrìguez Romàn & Gutierrez,

2010], equivalent to the length of an arm-and-a-half's length), or gestures, especially those we make with our hands and our head, which will assert the message we want to convey. If the officer uses these procedures, and the inmate keeps on showing a violent attitude, one of the techniques included in Comprehensive Penitentiary Defense will be applied. We must choose the most appropriate proportion of force for the specific situation.

To better understand the philosophy which gave rise to this style of self-defense, we will analyze each of its terms:

- **Comprehensive:** This system of self-defense comprises both physical and non-physical self-defense techniques. The physical techniques comprise a selection of different martial arts techniques, and thus constitute both a global and utilitarian approach to the martial arts. From this repertoire the most appropriate techniques are selected to employ in order to resolve a variety of situations.

- **Penitentiary:** Situations of disruption unique to the prison environment require rapid, efficient, and proportionate resolution. The solutions applicable in other, more general systems are usually insufficient or inappropriate, as they are not framed within the context of prison reality.

- **Defense:** The prison officer should always seek to avoid conflict through the use of the least harmful techniques possible in order to achieve successful resolution of situations where order has been disrupted.

There is a protocol of action from the General Secretariat for Penitentiary Institutions (*Secretaría General de Instituciones Penitenciarias*) regarding self-defense. This protocol was made by a group of prison officers who are martial arts experts. This group of experts have been training all the self-defense coaches who, in turn, regularly conduct training courses for all the staff in penitentiary centers. The aim of this training is to provide the officer with a proper knowledge of the correct use of the means of coercion. Coercive measures envisaged under the law include temporary isolation, personal physical force, rubber truncheons, appropriate aerosol sprays, and handcuffs. Under no circumstances is the use of firearms permitted. Instruments of coercion are kept in the place or places the governor considers most appropriate, and thus a prison officer never carries any coercive measure except his or her own physical strength.

It should be borne in mind that, even though the officers must pass several exams related to prison legislation and penal code (besides a very exhaustive medical examination), they are not required to show any knowledge of martial arts or self-defense. It is therefore crucial that they have continuous updating in these matters, either through courses organized by the Ministry of Internal Affairs (*Ministerio de Interior*) or through their personal training in any sports center where these disciplines are taught.

So, the prison professionals will apply the most adequate techniques in every conflict situation in which they may get involved. The technique will be chosen based on its proportionality towards the incident to be solved. We will not apply the same solution to passive resistance (refusal to obey prison officers' orders in the execution of their duties) as to active resistance (inmate's use of physical force to refuse to comply to orders or to oppose the action of the officers), and likewise we will not use the same technique to respond to a free-hand attack as when responding to an attack with cold steel. In addition, we will not use the same techniques to settle a fight between unarmed inmates as to solve a fight in which contenders are using pointed weapons.

The prison officers are not special intervention units, as are the Special Group of Operations (*Grupo Especial de Operaciones*, GEO) of the National Police Corps (*Cuerpo Nacional de Policía*), or the Special Intervention Unit (*Unidad Especial de Intervención*, UEI) of the Civil Guard. These two special units are the Spanish equivalent to the American SWAT. Nevertheless, the officer must know, day by day, how to solve, rapidly and with proportionality, any kind of altercation that might arise. Where such disruptions are serious, involving imminent danger to people or facilities, prison security forces may provisionally impose order when requested to do so by the governor. These special units have been properly trained to successfully face extremely dangerous situations. Their staff is specialized in negotiation skills for these kinds of situations. They only act when the path of dialog is no longer open.

The prison officers, on the other hand, have to be acquainted with skills of conflict resolution and must apply them from the very first moment of disruption of safety. Furthermore, using procedures as closely observing the inmates, they will try to anticipate the arising of the problem. Knowing each inmate individually is an invaluable weapon.

Prison officers are responsible for the internal security of the prison center. External security is in charge of national enforcement bodies: National Police Corps and Civil Guard.

The prison environment is a controlled environment: inmates are thoroughly frisked before they can come into the center, which makes impossible to find firearms inside. Nevertheless, it is possible to find handmade weapons, made from a variety of objects, such a section of a broom or mop handle, a shard of glass with a bandage or some plastic for the handle, a filed toothbrush handle hardened over a flame, a latch, the flashing or frame of a window, or the metal mounting of a fluorescent light shaped like a dagger.

In Comprehensive Penitentiary Defense, the gradual use of force is always considered. This force will be applied in crescendo, based on the resistance we find from the inmate when applying a technique, as while moving an inmate from one area to another inside the prison center. The inmate may collaborate or, on the contrary, may show passive, even active resistance. If the inmate collaborates, and based on their riskiness, they will be escorted by one to four officers.

If there is only one officer, he/she should walk behind the inmate, keeping a minimum safety distance. This way, the officer will have a perfect view of the inmate, and enough distance to repel any possible attack. On the other hand, the inmate will not be able to see the officer without turning their head. If the inmate is escorted by two officers, both of them will walk behind the inmate, making a triangle. If the inmate is particularly dangerous, and needs to be escorted by three officers, the third one will be placed in front of the inmate, ten feet away, so as to be able to repel any possible attack, even a kick. Should a fourth officer be necessary, this extra officer will go behind the main group, to form a triangle with the two officers that go behind the inmate. If the inmate offers passive resistance, we will apply a joint control of the inmate's arm (techniques 3, 4, or 9) and will walk on. If we face active resistance, we will apply techniques such as 10, 12, or 17 which, due to their fast implementation and high effectiveness, will leave no room for maneuver for the inmate to respond.

Through continuous training, the officer achieves the correct physical fitness and attitude to successfully face any disruption of safety. By being familiar with these kind of situations, the officer will know how to control these stressful situations caused by the inmates, and how to choose the best suited techniques to resolve them. The officer will be self-confident enough to be as effective as possible, causing the least possible damage.

Technique 1: The officer, placed behind the inmate, threads his arm between the side of the body and the left arm, raising this left arm. With his right arm, the officer sweeps the inmate's forearm to the right, and with his right hand, he holds the inmate's shoulder with the palm upwards. He rotates the inmate's forearm to increase the intensity of the technique.

Technique 2: The officer, placed behind the inmate, puts the truncheon horizontally starting from the front and working backwards, immobilizing the arm.

Technique 3: The officer, placed beside the inmate, holds the wrist with his outer hand and immobilizes the shoulder by twisting the elbow and pushing it against the solar plexus.

Technique 4: The officer, placed beside the inmate, holds the wrist with his outer hand and twists the elbow by threading his arm between the side of the body and the arm, and "tightens the knot of his tie."

Technique 5: Pressure on the base of the ear with index and middle fingers.
Technique 6: Pressure on the base of the ear with the knuckles of index and middle fingers.
Technique 7: Simultaneous pressure on the forearm and the inner side of the metacarpus.

Technique 8: Apply pressure on the central knuckles, while bending the wrist and using the armpit as a brace.

Technique 9: The Tray in one step.

Technique 10: The Tray in two steps. Suitable for subjects who offer more resistance or are more flexible.

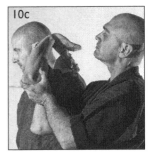

Technique 11: The Walk in the inmate's walking direction.

Technique 12: The Sleeping Cobra. We continue our walking direction.

Technique 13: Lapel hold. Simultaneous rotation of both elbows.

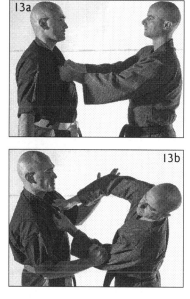

Technique 14: Lapel hold. Arm rotation and pressure on the armpit with central knuckles. Wrist twist.

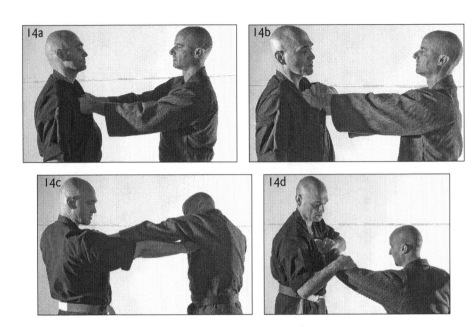

Technique 15: Lapel hold with the both hands. Thumb twist with the left hand. Wrist twist.

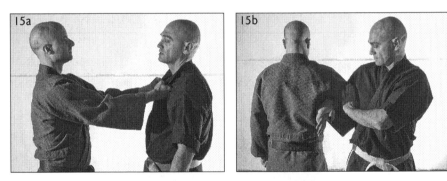

Technique 16: Front neck hold with both hands. The left hand holds and pulls down on the forearm, followed by a right hand bear hand strike to the face.

Technique 17: Wrist control and twist and subsequent elbow twist.

Technique 18: Handcuffing and elbow control.

Technique 19: Frontal attack with cold steel. After parrying the attack, wrist control and twist.

Technique 20: Frontal attack with cold steel. Right knife-hand strike to the wrist of the attacker with simultaneous attack to the side, and simultaneously taking his left forearm to the neck from the back. Lowers his position and twists the inmate's elbow over his bent leg.

Technique 21: Shove to the breast. The left hand holds the forearm. The right hand twists fingers vertically.

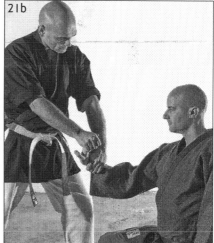

Technique 22: After twisting fingers vertically, elbow bending and subsequent control.

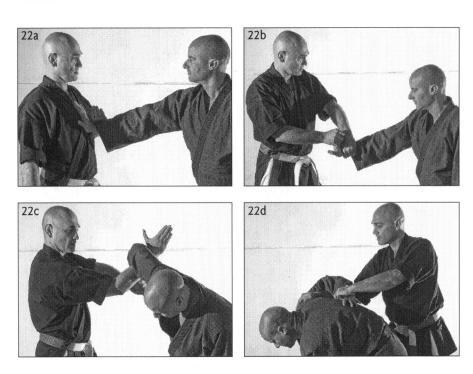

Technique 23: Circular frontal attack. Elbow control and twist with both hands.

Technique 24: Circular frontal attack. Knife-hand block to absorb the attack. Ridge-hand strike to the jaw followed by a strangulation hold.

Reference

Rodrìguez, Romàn, F.J., and Gutiérrez, Garcìa, C. (2010). Comprehensive Penitentiary Defense as developed for use in Spain. *Journal of Asian Martial Arts.* Volume 19(2): 46–71.

Acknowledgements

The author wishes to thank the following people: Julio César Benito Luengo (participation in the technical section); Mario Jiménez García (photography); Pedro Jorge Rodríguez Román (for translating).

· 8 ·

Changes in the Martial Artists Right to Bear Arms

by Peter Hobart, J.D.

Photograph © Marcel Braendli / 123RF.com

Many of those who study the various weapons systems of the Eastern martial arts are accustomed to carrying the tools of their trade to and from the training hall in their vehicles or on their persons, and keeping them in their homes. Increasingly, however, the mere possession of some of these same weapons has been criminalized, and being caught carrying many of them under circumstances that are not "manifestly lawful" certainly raises serious issues of criminal liability.

For example, the possession or carrying of a balisong—a gravity-operated folding knife that is a traditional Filipino weapon of self-defense—is now illegal in Australia, Canada, Britain, Switzerland, Germany, Hong Kong, and many American states. As a result, those who study and train with these so-called butterfly knives, often resort to using a special blunt and dull version of the weapon.

Generally speaking, weapons laws fall into three categories:

1) listed weapons
2) situational illegality, and
3) specific weapon bans.

Listed Weapons

The criminal laws of most jurisdictions have statutes describing classes of prohibited offensive weapons (or "POW" to police and prosecutors). The possession, carrying, or use of such weapons is generally considered criminal conduct per se. For example, in California, "[a]ny person in this state who . . . possesses . . . any ballistic knife . . . any nunchaku . . . any shuriken . . . any cane sword, any shobi-zue . . . or [c]oncealed upon his or her person any dirk or dagger . . . is punishable by imprisonment in a county jail not exceeding one year or in the state prison . . . ."[1]

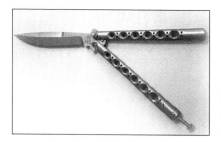 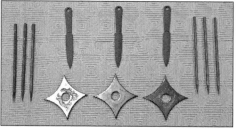

Butterfly knife photograph from Wikipedia.org

In Pennsylvania, offensive weapons are defined as, among other things, "[a]ny blackjack, sandbag, metal knuckles, dagger, knife, razor or cutting instrument, the blade of which is exposed in an automatic way by switch, push-button, spring mechanism, or otherwise, any stun gun, stun baton, taser or other electronic or electric weapon ...."[2]

In Arkansas, "[a] person commits the offense of carrying a weapon if he or she possesses . . . any bladed hand instrument that is capable of inflicting serious physical injury or death by cutting or stabbing . . . on or about his or her person, in a vehicle occupied by him or her, or otherwise readily available for use with a purpose to employ the handgun, knife, or club as a weapon against a person."[3]

In Iowa, "[a] person who goes armed with a knife concealed on or about the person, if the person does not use the knife in the commission of a crime.

. . [i]f the knife has a blade exceeding eight inches in length, commits an aggravated misdemeanor."[4]

In Montana, "[e]very person who carries or bears concealed upon his person a dirk, dagger . . . sword cane . . . knife having a blade 4 inches long or longer. . . or other deadly weapon shall be punished by a fine not exceeding $500 or imprisonment in the county jail for a period not exceeding 6 months, or both."[5]

Situational Illegality

In other jurisdictions, the legality of possessing certain weapons depends on the situation. These crimes are sometimes categorized as possession of instruments of crime (or "PIC" to police and prosecutors). In Florida, for example,"[i]f any person having or carrying any dirk, sword, sword cane . . . or other weapon shall, in the presence of one or more persons, exhibit the same in a rude, careless, angry, or threatening manner, not in necessary self-defense, the person so offending shall be guilty of a misdemeanor of the first degree . . . ."[6]

In Minnesota, "[w]hoever shall go armed with a dirk, dagger, sword, pistol, or other offensive and dangerous weapon, without reasonable cause to fear an assault or other injury or violence to person, family, or property, may, on complaint of any other person having reasonable cause to fear an injury or breach of the peace, be required to find sureties for keeping the peace, for a term not exceeding six months, with the right of appealing as before provided."[7]

In Mississippi, "[i]f any person, having or carrying any dirk, dirk-knife, sword, sword-cane, or any deadly weapon, or other weapon the carrying of which concealed is prohibited, shall, in the presence of three or more persons, exhibit the same in a rude, angry, or threatening manner, not in necessary self-defense, or shall in any manner unlawfully use the same in any fight or quarrel, the person so offending, upon conviction thereof, shall be fined in a sum not exceeding five hundred dollars or be imprisoned in the county jail not exceeding three months, or both."[8]

In Nevada, "a person having, carrying or procuring from another person any dirk, dirk-knife, sword, sword cane . . . or other deadly weapon, who, in the presence of two or more persons, draws or exhibits any of such deadly weapons in a rude, angry or threatening manner not in necessary self-defense, or who in any manner unlawfully uses that weapon in any fight or quarrel, is guilty of a misdemeanor."[9]

© Chaoss | Dreamstime.com

In Puerto Rico, "[a]ny person who without justified motive, uses against another person . . . ninja stars, knives, daggers, swords . . . or any other similar object that may be deemed to be a bladed weapon . . . or unsheathes, shows, or uses to commit or attempt to commit a crime, shall be guilty of a felony and upon conviction shall be punished with a penalty of imprisonment for a fixed term of three (3) years."[10]

In Washington, "[i]t shall be unlawful for any person to carry, exhibit, display, or draw any . . . dagger, sword, knife or other cutting or stabbing instrument . . . or any other weapon apparently capable of producing bodily harm, in a manner, under circumstances, and at a time and place that either manifests an intent to intimidate another or that warrants alarm for the safety of other persons."[11]

Pennsylvania law, for example, makes it a crime to possess, among other things, any "implement for the infliction of serious bodily injury which serves no common lawful purpose."[12] This definition turns in many ways on whether the weapon in question "serves a common lawful purpose." On this basis, the Pennsylvania Superior Court held that, "Though nunchaku sticks, which are short sticks of wood hinged end-to-end by a short cord, can be used offensively to inflict serious injury, in view of fact that student or instructor of the martial arts could have occasion to use the nunchaku in the peaceful practice of karate exercises and because karate is practiced as a sport and exercise by many citizens of the Commonwealth, nunchaku sticks are not an 'offensive weapon' within meaning of this section."[13]

© Zuperpups | Dreamstime.com

Weapons Bans

In some jurisdictions, specific legislation has been enacted to criminalize the possession of a particular weapon. Britain's ban on "samurai swords" in 2008 is a notable example. With the widespread availability of firearms in the United States, edged-weapon crimes are understandably somewhat less common, at least in a relative sense, but one need look no further than our English cousins to find chilling examples of the ways in which the katana—the Japanese long sword—can be used to ends that are every bit as lethal as the gun's.

On January 28, 2000, Nigel Jones, a member of the British Parliament, and his assistant, Andrew Pennington, were meeting with constituents in their Cheltenham office. Without warning, one of those constituents, Rob Ashman, produced a katana from beneath his black overcoat and attacked them. Jones and Pennington tried to fight off the six-foot Ashman. Jones sustained severe cuts to both hands and arms. Pennington was killed. The autopsy revealed that he had been stabbed at least six times and that most of his internal organs had been sliced open.[14]

A report released by the British Home Office in 2007 estimated that there had been at least one hundred crimes involving what the government referred to as "samurai swords" in England since 2003, many of them resulting in fatalities.[15]

As a result of this horrific wave of violence, a sword ban went into effect in England in 2008. Swords with the characteristics of a katana were added to the Offensive Weapons Order, and the penalty for being found in possession of one is a jail sentence of up to six months and a fine as high as £5,000. Exceptions exist for bona fide martial arts practitioners and collectors, but the risks of ensuring that your school and your sword are eligible for such "defenses" is apparent. Suffice it to say that the days when British students could take the train to the dojo with their swords slung across their backs are likely a thing of the past.

What of the United States then—the home of the right to bear arms? In addition to listed weapons and situational crimes described above, outright bans on particular weapons are also not unprecedented, but resistance is fierce. In 2009, for example, U.S. Customs and Border Protection Services announced a possible change to the definition of "switchblade knife"—a class of weapon already banned by the 1958 act of the same name—and the outcry from various quarters was immediate and persistent. In fact, so vocal was this opposition that legislation was proposed in Congress to block the expansion of the existing definition.[16] And while this particular battle may have been averted for the time being, the war on weapons is far from over, both at home and abroad.

Conclusion

The laws presented above are by no means an exhaustive list of the weapons crimes and defenses that currently exist in the statutes of the several states and elsewhere. Even if they were, the law of weapons is subject to change, and the application of these laws depends in large part upon the exercise of discretion by police and prosecutors. Conduct that might warrant only a warning in one instance could result in serious jail time and a permanent criminal conviction in another.

The purpose of this chapter is not to provide a comprehensive guide to the nuances of weapons law in every jurisdiction. Rather, its aim is to raise awareness on the part of martial artists—particularly those entrusted with teaching their art to others—that we live in a different world from the one in which many of us cut our martial teeth. What were once dismissed as relatively harmless playground fights or instances of drunken high jinx can now trigger significant criminal and civil consequences. Martial arts tools, and even toys, may now be considered dangerous illegal weapons, landing those who merely possess them in serious trouble. And even if those possessing such instruments are eventually exonerated, the process of wending one's way through the criminal justice system is cumbersome and fairly unpleasant to those on the receiving end.

What lessons, then, can the martial artist draw from this survey of the state of the law, in order to protect himself and his students?

1) Listed Weapons: First and foremost, any martial artist who practices with weapons should become familiar with the listed prohibited weapons in his particular jurisdiction, and be aware that even if there exists an exception for martial arts training, any police officer who sees someone in possession of a listed weapon can, and probably should, stop that person, and make further inquiries.

2) Situational Illegality: Laws regarding situational illegality, on the other hand, tend to require proof that the person possessed the particular instrument with the intent to use it criminally. This is typically determined by some combination of the nature of the item (e.g., pipe gun); any modifications made to the item (a homemade silencer); and the circumstances under which it is possessed (carried by someone loitering in an alley at night). As a result, even when dealing with weapons that are not illegal per se, the responsible martial artist should be aware of the circumstances under which he is carrying or using his training weapons, and take care that his actions and appearance are consistent with lawful use.

3) Bona Fide Martial Arts Use: Many, if not most, jurisdictions permit martial artists to possess and practice with the tools of their trade. Yet it must be considered that anyone can claim to be a martial artist. The key is distinguishing between "wannabes" and serious students of the martial arts. In addition to your behavior, carrying some kind of identification affiliating you with a legitimate martial arts school when transporting your weapon(s) is probably a good idea.

4) Weapons versus Training Equipment: The less common a weapon is in conventional martial arts training, the harder it is to justify its possession. It is no accident that sword-canes appear on the prohibited weapons list of most jurisdictions. There are very few schools that teach the use of this weapon, and it is therefore a safe bet that those possessing such an item do so more for use as a weapon than as a training tool.

5) Transporting versus Carrying: The law in most states permits weapons enthusiasts to transport their tools to and from their place of practice, sometimes in specific types of containers. There is thus a significant difference between the way the law would view someone driving to the dojo with his katana in a locked case in the trunk of his car and someone else routinely carrying a knife on his belt "for self-defense purposes."

6) Carrying Concealed: On a related note, there is often a difference in the eyes of the law between mere possession and "carrying concealed." While it might seem somewhat counterintuitive, slinging one's sword bag over the shoulder for all to see may be viewed as less threatening than concealing the same weapon under a long coat.

7) Be Circumspect: Just as a police officer is trained not to draw his weapon unless he intends to use it, a professional martial artist shows a healthy respect for the tools of his trade. It is wise not to draw any unnecessary attention to the weapon being carried, no matter how tempting it might be to show it off, and as discussed above, sometimes the brandishing of a weapon can transform legal possession into illegal conduct.

8) An Ounce of Prevention: Given that weapons laws are often subject to interpretation, and police and prosecutors have wide discretion in that regard, it is worth considering making a trip to your local police station to introduce yourself and your art, and seek guidance regarding the applicable laws.

9) Self-Defense: Should a legitimate martial arts practitioner happen to be attacked while armed with his weapon, conventional self-defense and lethal force rules apply. There can be little doubt, however, that use of a katana or similar martial arts weapon would be considered "deadly force," triggering the higher standards that often apply in this context.

THE THREE CARDINAL RULES REGARDING THE USE OF FORCE

- **Duty to Retreat**—In some jurisdictions, the victim must "retreat to the wall if it is safe to do so" before using lethal force in self-defense.
- **Unclean Hands**—In some jurisdictions the victim is not entitled to use lethal force in self-defense unless he has "clean hands," meaning he did not provoke, continue, or escalate the confrontation.
- **Proportionality**—In almost every jurisdiction and context, the victim is only entitled to use the amount of force that appears reasonably necessary to protect himself from that degree of force with which he is imminently threatened.

---

10) Real versus Toy Swords: Finally, another counterintuitive phenomenon illustrated by the British sword ban is that a "real" sword—either made before 1954 or forged in the traditional manner—which is clearly a more fearsome weapon than the cheap replicas that have become increasingly available to the public, is likelier to be deemed a legitimate and therefore legal tool of the trade for the martial arts professional.

*The foregoing survey of the laws of various jurisdictions
is merely intended to provide general guidance for the
professional martial arts practitioner. It should not be relied
upon as a specific defense in either criminal or civil court.
All photographs courtesy of the author, except where noted.*

Notes

1 California Penal Code § 12020 (But note that subdivision (a) does not apply to any of the following ... The possession of a nunchaku on the premises of a school which holds a regulatory or business license and teaches the arts of self-defense).
2 Title 18 Pennsylvania Consolidated Statutes Annotated § 908.
3 Arkansas Code § 5-73-120.
4 Iowa Code Annotated § 724.4.
5 Montana Code Annotated 45-8-316.
6 Florida Statutes Annotated § 790.10.
7 Minnesota Statutes Annotated § 625.16.
8 Mississippi Code Annotated § 97-37-19.
9 Nevada Revised Statutes Annotated § 202.320.
10 Title 25 Laws of Puerto Rico Annotated § 458d-1.
11 Revised Code of Washington Annotated § 9.41.270.
12 Title 18 Pennsylvania Consolidated Statutes Annotated § 908.
13 Commonwealth Adams, 369 A.2d 479 (Pa. Super. Ct. 1976).
14 Terror Sword Attack on MP, *The Mirror*, January 29, 2000.
15 Examples of sword violence in Britain forming the basis for the sword ban:
    • April 2000, Paul Horgan murders his girlfriend in their East London flat by slashing her forty-four times with "a three foot samurai sword."
    • December 2001, Daniel Jethoo of Enfield, North London, kills Bradley Knight with a katana while Knight is walking home from a Christmas party.
    • January 2002, Scotsman Robert Forbes stabs John Potts to death, striking him almost fifty times with a "samurai warrior's sword."
    • June 2002, Richard Markham flees the United Kingdom with police hot on his trail for killing and dismembering a former friend at his home in Basingstoke.
    • January 2003, Jason Kelly, a teenage member of a street gang, kills Robert Dunn with a single thrust of a "samurai sword" in the middle of a busy street in Middlesbrough.
    • November 2003, Daniel Leather kills his own father using not one but two "samurai swords."

- May 2004, John Cook of County Antrim is found dead in a pool of blood, his arm severed by a razor-sharp sword.
- July 2005, Bradely Moran killed Matthew Stiling by stabbing him with an "18 inch samurai sword" during a gang fight in the seaside resort of Sidmouth.
- May 2006, Carie Burns of County Durham dies of stab wounds inflicted by Hugh Penrose with a Japanese sword.
- September 2006, Barry Stone stabs his girlfriend, Nicola Sutton, to death at their apartment in Cheshire, using "a samurai sword."
- June 2007, Julian Mayfield-Sparks kills his brother, Corin, with a katana.

[16] Bid to expand knife ban doesn't cut it with critics, *Washington Times*, June 24, 2009.

index

Made in the USA
Coppell, TX
11 September 2021

62164001R00072